Jasmine Moran's Scottish Family Tartan.

The Path I Chose

In My Own Words

OKLAHOMA HALL *of* FAME

P U B L I S H I N G

ISBN: 978-1-938923-37-1

Library of Congress Control Number: 2018933392

Book and Cover Design by photogDESIGN.com
Printed in Canada

1400 Classen Drive
Oklahoma City, Oklahoma 73106
405.235.4458
www.OklahomaHoF.com

OKLAHOMA HALL *of* FAME

BOARD OF DIRECTORS

OKLAHOMA VOICES SERIES

The Path I Chose

In My Own Words

by Jasmine Moran

with Karen Anson

Foreword by Robert Henry

Series Editor: Gini Moore Campbell

OKLAHOMA HALL *of* FAME

PUBLISHING

TABLE OF CONTENTS

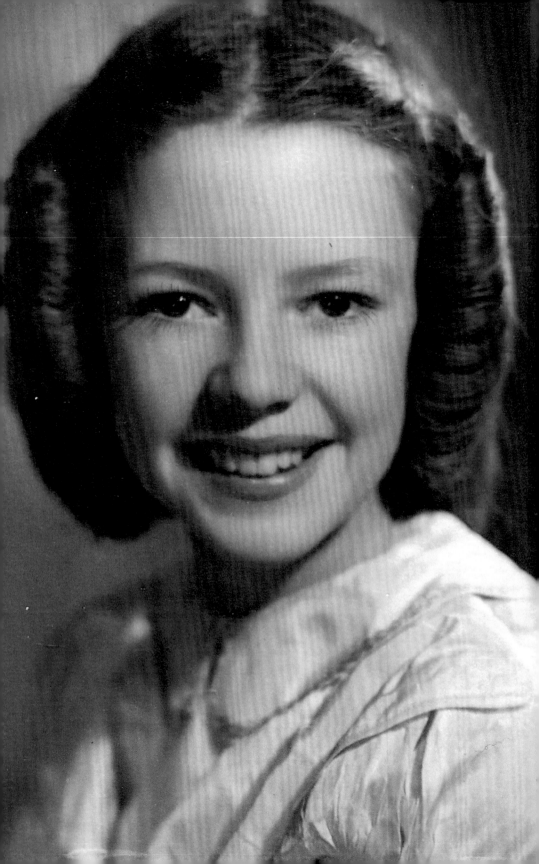

FOREWORD

By Robert Henry

A couple of days after I met Jasmine Moran, she became my mother-in-law. And she was a great one. People paid to see it.

I shall never forget that meeting—at an audition for the Shawnee Little Theatre production of *A Man for All Seasons*, Robert Bolt's immortal play picturing the best side of Sir/Saint Thomas More. Jasmine was cast for the role she sought, Alice More, the beloved and long-suffering wife of Sir Thomas. Striving to be More, I ended up as William Roper, a Lutheran willing to change spots to marry More's daughter, Meg. Several weeks of rehearsal and performance, oft attended by Jasmine's husband (driver, confidant, and friend) Melvin, cemented a friendship that has lasted almost 40 years, and will never end.

The title to Bolt's play was borrowed from Robert Whittington, a contemporary of Thomas More who observed that More was "a man of wit and learning; of gentleness, lowliness, affability; of mirth and pastimes; and sometimes of sad gravity: a man for all seasons."

And in my view, Jasmine Moran is a woman for all seasons. Lord knows she's seen a lot of them: growing up with a single mom during a desperate world war; observing the Battle of Britain in literally front row seats; surviving, during that war, forced foster homes, scarlet fever, and pneumonia; overcoming dyslexia; acting in a youthful career on the road and in the British stage throughout the country; and, forsaking all she had and knew (except the most important thing, Melvin) to create a remarkable life in her new country, the United States, and eventually her new city, Seminole, Oklahoma.

Jasmine Moran is a truly lovely, but in many ways, a very private person, who for some reason very frankly tells almost all in this captivating autobiography. As in Bolt's and Whittington's observations about Thomas More, there are, herein, tales of learning and certainly wit; stories of gentleness (especially as to God's little creatures); stories both of mirth and gravity. Through them all, having left family, friends, country, and religion for her new life in Oklahoma, there is Jasmine Lindsay Moran, a woman for all the seasons she has confronted with courage, dignity, and Scottish wit.

Did I say Scottish? Assuredly, for Bonnie Scotland was the home of Jasmine's ancestors, and, as the reader will see, mystic Scottish traits and talents stayed with Jasmine all her life. Her mother, Lilian, whom I had the great fortune to meet, had both a Scottish brogue and Scottish bravura that certainly put steel into Jasmine's soul. (Lilian, I must note, could cut to the chase. I am grateful for her one word description of the Wonder Bread that we suffered through in this country before we remembered how to bake bread: "guck.")

Jasmine's life during the war makes up a remarkable portion of this book. On the ground during the Battle of Britain, Jasmine recalled the greatness of the British Bulldog Winston Churchill whose powerful prose and dogged determination may be the reason the allies prevailed in World War II. Jasmine's mom actually met Churchill, and

I am certain they intuited that each other possessed the same traits of truth, loyalty, and dependability that are the essential traits of this entire story. Jasmine explains how the bombings were so constant and threatening that all sorts of strategies had to be developed to avoid mass extermination.

Now Jasmine admits that she has not always been 100% truthful. She, well, lied about her age in order to perform in theatre. Traveling the width and breadth of Britain, without family, and at her age of fifteen is an adventure hard to even fathom in today's society.   She acted, sang, and danced with many of legend including: the glass-and-racial-ceiling breaking Muriel Smith ("Bloody Mary" in *South Pacific*); Mary Martin (later of *Peter Pan* fame); Millicent Martin (star of *Alfie* and of television as Gertrude Moon in *Frasier*); and Sean Connery (who believe it or not, was at this point a dual role playing minor parts.) Millicent Martin and Jasmine have remained friends; indeed, I will long treasure hearing them sing a duet together at a recent presentation of the eponymous "Jasmine Award," the award given by the fantastical Jasmine Moran Children's Museum to those who, in the Museum's view, have specially cared for the children of our state and world.

Although I was fascinated by her life as an itinerant actor, I must admit I was in a bit of a hurry to hear her side of how she and Melvin met and came together. I won't share the drenching details here and now, but I simply observe, thank God for second dates….

I would also add, thank God for wonderful mothers-in-law, as Jasmine credits Melvin's strong—willed but gentle and understanding mother as being a probable reason for her marrying him! Not that Jasmine's mother Lilian was silent on the issue: "Let me tell you, if I were you, I'd marry him." Could both mothers be wrong?

I must comment, though, on another lovable trait of Jasmine

that animates her story. Lovable, indeed, for she is one of the most dedicated animal lovers I have ever known. This part of Judaism certainly came naturally to Jasmine, for as Proverbs 12:10 pointedly notes, the righteous know the souls of their animals. Jasmine has adopted more cats and dogs than the Pied Piper, and she has even been known to sic the law on those who are cruel to those our Native American friends fondly term the " four leggeds." The wrath of a righteous Scottish woman is to be avoided!

The Seminole years are dominated by the most important things in Jasmine's and Melvin's life, their children, and their community. As to her children, Elisa, David, and Marilyn, who are predictably outstanding, Jasmine correctly gives the greatest praise a Jewish mother could offer. "Because they have dedicated their lives to helping others, I proudly believe they are my most significant contribution to society." Could any mother hope for more?

And Seminole would foster another great relationship that has helped to repair the world, a lifelong friendship first with young David, and then with David and Molly Boren. The Borens and Morans have certainly not left the world as they found it, and the remarkable things they have done together could not have easily been done separately.

And speaking of things remarkable, Jasmine's path toward her eponymous museum also receives important mention. This gift that she and Melvin have given the world is second to none I know of in philanthropy. My own children, Rachel and Josh, have spent many an hour in this center of creativity. Indeed, Rachel was, I believe, the first contributor to name a brick after her hamster, Marbles. We knew that Jasmine would approve!

In this wonderful story, Jasmine readily admits to being judgmental, opinionated, unrepentant, temperamental (or Scotch), and unashamedly so: "When I form an opinion, sometimes it takes years to find out why I feel that way, but I find that I am usually right." I know that I, and I suspect Melvin, have also found that to be the case!

Of course, as her story further reveals, Jasmine is also loving and kind, wise and caring, a giver of joy, a guardian of animals, a teacher of children. In fact, I still like to think of her as my mother-in-law; not only was she convincing in that role, to this day, like her many friends, I welcome her motherly advice and opinions.

ACKNOWLEDGMENTS

by Jasmine Moran

The Children's Museum has become much more special than any of us ever envisioned. Our initial board was created in October, 1988. Not one of our initial board members, other than Melvin and I, had ever visited or even heard of a children's museum. We did not know what we were doing. I truly believe that God wanted this museum to succeed and he helped us every step of the way. I believe that God, along with Dale Donaho, brought Marci Donaho from Arizona to Oklahoma to provide the leadership we needed.

I want to thank all of our donors for their gifts of money, time, gifts, and things. And I wish to express appreciation to them individually by name. I compiled the names, as best I could, and discovered there were a thousand individuals, companies, corporations, and other entities who have supported the museum in various ways. Because of the number of wonderful and generous supporters, I'll only list a small percent by name. And I hope everyone will understand that their generous help was sincerely appreciated. Without these wonderful individuals and entities, the Children's Museum would not exist.

The museum has had fantastic leadership. Board presidents

were Marci Donaho, Lana Reynolds, Karen James, Jim Cook, Harry Coates, Kenneth Henderson, Amy Colclazier, Ray McQuiston, and, presently, Marci. Ray McQuiston is now board chairman.

Tommy Mills was the museum's first executive director. He did a fine job. He was succeeded by Marci in June, 1996. Our Board of Trustees consists of 120 Oklahomans from throughout the state. Among our board members are present and past Oklahoma Governors, U.S. Senators, Congressman, Legislators, additional elected office holders, many college presidents, etc. Since the museum opened in January, 1993, every Oklahoma First Lady has served on our board.

So many to thank: When we planned a new healthcare exhibit, Stan Hupfeld, former INTEGRIS CEO, and First Lady Kim Henry raised $500,000 from INTEGRIS, Mercy, OU Medical Center, Saint Francis, and SSM Health. And, Governor Brad Henry and Kim hosted the hospital CEOs at a luncheon in the Governor's Mansion for the purpose of thanking them for helping the Children's Museum.

Every other year the museum honors a person or a couple for the purpose of publicly thanking them for what they have done for young people. Our honorees have been Cathy Keating, David and Molly Boren, Gene Rainbolt, Kim Henry, George and Donna Nigh, Barry Switzer, Robert Henry, Burns and Ann Hargis, Bart Conner and Nadia Comaneci, and Mike and Susan Turpen. These wonderful people have all been honored before. Yet, they graciously allowed us to honor them because the events raised money for the purpose of assisting the museum and providing admission scholarships. I thank every one of them and I want to express appreciation to Governor Mary Fallin for her welcome addresses at many of these events. George Nigh, our emcee-in-chief, has emceed all of our tribute events except our first, Mike Turpen and Burns Hargis emceed and Robert Henry emceed the event when George and Donna were honored.

Almost every major Oklahoma Foundation has helped us including Mabee, Zarrow, Kirkpatrick, Schusterman, Whitten-Newman, Sarkeys, and many, many more. Two-hundred companies have contributed including AT&T, BancFirst, Sonic, Cox Communications, Conoco-Phillips, Chesapeake Energy, Kerr-McGee, and so many others. Donald W. Reynolds Foundation is the sponsor of the Oklahoma Museum Network, which includes the Children's Museum. Also, we have had so much assistance from the Chickasaw Nation, Gordon Cooper Technology Center, Oklahoma Energy Resources Board, and Seminole State College.

The Children's Museum building was initially a 20,000-square-foot building used to repair oilfield drilling rigs. The building was cleaned by volunteers and genius contractor, Keith Shaw, transformed the building into a 20,000-square-foot children's museum. Following numerous expansions, the museum now has 40,000 square feet of indoor exhibit space. Thank you so much, Keith! Murals throughout the museum were painted by Marilyn Fulton, Teri Hooten, April Jones, Kelly Haney, and other local artists. Richard Fulton constructed our elaborate dollhouse and electric train exhibit. When the museum needs additional assistance, a call to Seminole State College brings out college athletic teams to direct traffic, stuff and hide eggs for the annual egg hunt, or other assistance that might be needed. Incidentally, our Easter Bunny is named Shirlene Cofer. When "heavy lifting" is needed, a call to Wrangler brings out all the help we need. Thank you, Seminole State College and thank you, Ray McQuiston and Wrangler!

So many individuals have helped us. Years ago I served on the board of the Oklahoma Arts Institute. Fellow board member, Ted d'Andriole, a Southwestern Bell executive, became a friend. Since then every Southwestern Bell/AT&T Oklahoma president has served on our museum board.

My lifelong friend, actress Millicent Martin (Mrs. Moon on *Frasier*), flew into Oklahoma City, at her own expense, to sing at our tribute event honoring Bart and Nadia.

A partial list of individuals, not previously mentioned, who have given the museum so much of their time and treasure includes Ann Alspaugh, Bill Anoatubby, Karen Anson, Jari Askins, Jimmie Austin, Janice Banks, Bonnie Battles, Ann Biddy, Joyce Boggs, Dan Boren, Michelle and Larry Briggs, Amy Britt, Eddie Coates, Janene Day, Nance Diamond, Dale Donaho, Mike Dundee, Zora and Jim Fowler, Mary Frates, Craig Froelich, Don Gill, Claudean Greene, Liz Gunter, Shelley and Jim Hamby, Donna Hardin, Kay and John Hargrave, Rose and Kenneth Henderson, Jan Henry, Kenny Howard, Betty Huckabay, Theresa Jones, Barbara and Bob Jones, Rebecca Kennedy, Kelly Kirk, Ken Levit, Cai Levy, Jane Lodes, Phyllis and Guy Logsdon, Lana and Dave Lopez, Ann Lott, Tim Mathews, Mike McCreight, Tom McDaniel, Gordon Melson, Frank Merrick, Sandy and Stewart Meyers, Vivian Mills, Vickie Moran, Doyle Morris, Ron Norick, Steve Owens, Pam Parks, Isla Mae Phillips, Laurie and Jay Phillips, Hope Pickering, Tom Price, Betty Price, Liz Robertson, Lelani and Dennis Roesler, Steve Saxon, Mark Schell, Lisa and Steve Schoaps, Jimmie Smart, Betty Smith, Larry Smith, Sue Snodgrass, Tom Swearingen, Mary Gordon Taft, Donna and Ivan Terry, Mike Terry, Kathy Thorley, Karrie and Jim Utterback, Reggie Whitten, Steve Williams, David Wilson, and Darla Zuhdi.

I would also like to thank my children (Marilyn Moran-Townsend and Bill Townsend, Elisa Moran and Gary Kleiman, David Moran and Kris Olsson), and the many, many volunteers and wonderful staff for their support, love, and encouragement.

I am blessed to have seen the opening of our Animal Shelter. I especially want to thank Keith, Sassy, and Charity Shaw, City Manager

Steve Saxon, City Council members (with special thanks to D.D. Patterson), The Seminole Humane Society, and, especially, Mary Ann Hill, Marta Mattingly, and Jamie Mills. The shelter staff and volunteers are wonderful, amazing, and caring.

This book is dedicated to the man in my life, my husband, Melvin, who gave me a safe and happy life, a wonderful and loving family with three terrific children who fill my heart with pride.

And a final thank you to a dear inspiring, supportive lady, Karen Anson, without whom this book would never have been finished. Karen, you are an amazing friend. Mel and I love and admire you.

ACKNOWLEDGMENTS

by Karen Anson

Karen Anson is a graduate of New Lima (Oklahoma) High School and Seminole State College. She also attended the University of Oklahoma and spent more than 20 years as an editor at *The Seminole Producer*. She has been published in *Oklahoma Today* and by the *Associated Press*. The Oklahoma Hall of Fame published her biography of Melvin Moran, *Moving Heaven and Earth: The Life of Melvin Moran*, and *The Impossible Dream: A History of the Jasmine Moran Children's Museum*. Anson lives in Seminole with her husband, Jerry. They have three adult children and five grandsons.

When Jasmine Moran asked me to help her with her life story, she said it had been an amazing journey. I found that she was right and so it was no surprise that writing that story was also amazing. Over the span of four years, I sat in Jasmine's kitchen at a bow window overlooking the wildlife—teeming back garden and listened to stories of war, fame, love, and philanthropy. Jasmine wanted the book written in her own words. Her own British vernacular is so much more charming than my American English so I became more of an editor instead of an author. The research I did to fill in a few of her vague memories enriched a whole period of history for me.

The beauty of those golden afternoons won't soon be forgotten. Her stories were interspersed with private concerts as she sang me songs from her past, and poetry recitals as she remembered words that had inspired and comforted her throughout her 80-plus years. And everyday at four, tea.

Thank you, Jasmine, for sharing your life with me, for trusting me to gently craft your sentences for accuracy and clarity, and most of all for your generosity. You will forever be more than a subject to me—a beloved and loving friend.

ANTECEDENTS

Chapter 1

I'm a talker. I come from a long line of talkers. My mother and my great-grandmother were both very good storytellers. My mother was wonderful. Lilian Davina Low was of Scottish descent, and throughout history, storytelling was an art to the Gaelic people. So she was good at spinning tales.

Mother would make up bedtime stories for the children, wonderful stories, for my kids and her other grandchildren. We taped some, but we didn't get them all. I wish we had.

Mother would hear something and it would strike a bell. She would start with something like, "Thelma was a good girl who lived in the woods, she had parents but most of her time was spent in the woods. She made friends with the bunnies and squirrels. They all waited for her to come down in the morning."

There were always little animals running around in her stories. She was quite a weaver of tales. She always tried to interject something important, like being kind to animals or others, or appreciating what God gives us. That would be the basis, and then she would go on from there. In her stories when the girl was seated telling stories to the rabbits, fish kept popping up and then having to go back down to get local doctor, taking care of people. New babies are almost always night calls.

When a prospective father came for her, she would have to go with him immediately. If she was making dinner, she had to leave. Everything was an emergency. When she was away, one of the children, usually the oldest, Agnes, had to feed the family.

Then maybe there was a five-mile trek back to the house afterward. When Great-Grandmother would come home, maybe she had just seen a baby die or some such tragedy, and this was probably on her mind, but still she had to take care of the children. It couldn't have been easy for any of them.

There were harsh winters. It was a cold rugged place. And Great-Grandfather had to keep the boat repaired and cleaned; it was necessary to keep food on the table.

There was always a shortness of money, but not food. They always had food, but were not always able to purchase things like shoes and coats. So hand-me-downs were used until worn out. They all had to work. They were aware that they were poor.

What fish Great-Grandfather could not sell, he brought home and they had it for supper. They lived on fish 99% of the time. The family used to long for something else besides fish. They'd say, "We had fish for supper last night." Great-Grandmother would say, "Well, you're having it again tonight." Marjory was all of five feet tall and had a temper. The children all behaved when she got angry.

Marjory was also a suffragette, which got her into a lot of trouble. She chained herself to a lamp post and threw away the key. The police couldn't get her unlocked, so they beat her up and, when they got her freed, they dragged her off to jail. She was so mad at her husband for not coming down to bail her out that she wouldn't cook for a week. So you see I come from tough stock.

Scotland's first suffrage groups appeared in the late 1860s, demanding the vote in order to improve women's lives. The suffragists used peaceful, legal tactics to try to win support, sending petitions to Parliament, writing letters, distributing leaflets, and organizing meetings. They sought to win equal rights through discussion and debate.

However, after thirty years of peaceful campaigning produced only minor change, suffragettes became more militant. They wanted the same things as the suffragists, but were prepared to break the law and go to prison for their beliefs. Scottish suffragettes chained themselves to railings, smashed windows, and slashed portraits of King Edward VII. They set fire to important buildings and, when they went to prison, often refused to eat. Authorities tried to force-feed them, provoking a public outcry. In 1918, Parliament passed The Representation of the People Act, a law stating that all women over the age of 30 could vote. In 1928, they gave full voting rights to all women over the age of 21. - bbc.com

When the Lows' last born daughter, Edith Alice, was 19 or 20, she became pregnant out of wedlock. When Marjory found her daughter was pregnant, she was furious. She was even more furious when she found out who the father was. Donald Stuart MacPhee was a soldier in the army and, by the time he found out his fiancée was expecting, he was already back in India with his unit. In 1910, you didn't fly home for compassionate leave. He was writing to her from India. They were engaged. He had no idea she was pregnant. A friend came home for his mother's funeral and, when he returned to India, he told Donald, who took the first ship back to Scotland. He picked up a minister as soon as he got off the troop ship. He went straight to the hospital to marry Edith. But her mother, Marjory, wouldn't let him in to her daughter's room.

My mother, Lilian Davina Low, was born April 15, 1910 in Perth, Scotland. Her mother, Edith, died two weeks later, April 30,

1910, of milk fever, never knowing that Donald had come all the way to Scotland to marry her. He was never allowed to see his baby, my mother. He sent money for my mother to be raised. Although her grandmother never let her see her father, Mother later took his last name, MacPhee.

When my mother's father returned to India, he met someone else and married her and had two daughters by her. He did well in the service, and was awarded several medals. Later he returned to Scotland. During World War II, his daughters distinguished themselves in the Women's Army Corps.

On Christmas night when my mother was about a year old, there was a knock at the door. Nobody was there, except a child all wrapped in a blanket in a basket in the snow. There was a note, saying something like, "This child is two months old and I can't take care of her."

Jasmine Moran's sister, Davina, drew a composite of their mother, grandmother, and great-grandmother in pencil, which Jasmine displays in her home in Seminole. Pictured front to back are her mother Lilian Davina MacPhee Burchell; grandmother Edith Alice Low, who died two weeks after baby Lilian was born; and her great-grandmother, Marjory Kay Fisher Low.

Instead of turning the baby in, Marjory, my mother's grandmother, decided to keep her. They called her Georgina, Ina for short. Ina and Mother were raised together. My mother's father gave part of his pension for Mother to be raised, but the money was used to raise both children. When Ina's feet grew, she got the shoes first and Mother got the second-hand shoes even though they used her father's money to buy them. Naturally my mother grew resentful.

Jasmine's great-grandmother Marjory Low is pictured above with another of her granddaughters, Marjorie Burns. They enjoyed a warm relationship, Jasmine said, unlike the relationship between Marjory Low and Jasmine's mother, Lilian.

After school all the children had to have a job to help pay the bills. In the town of Perth, there was an establishment, where they dyed and cleaned clothes. It was a very large business called Pullen's. Most of the family went to work there. Mother didn't because she was very short. When she first started working, she was 12 or 13. All the other workers had to reach the big dye vats and pour chemicals into the dye. Then they would press the clothes, roll the hot roller type presses, and a mangle that gets all the moisture out; yes, a wringer. Anyway most of Mother's siblings did that.

Mother couldn't work at Pullen's because she was too short. So her Granny put her to work for a farmer, milking cattle. She said, "I could reach the udders so I earned my money that way." As it turned out, it was the best thing that could have happened to her.

Years later, we figured out that most of her aunts and uncles died of upper respiratory and sinus problems, mostly cancer, because they were all working with the chemicals, which were not under any government control. There was nothing to take the pollution out of the air and they were breathing that for hours every day. Nobody realized why so many died young until many years later.

Although life was hard, there were some high points. Mother attended church with a portion of the Royal Family, who lived in Perth at the time. She saw Lady Elizabeth Bowes-Lyon and all the Royal Family at the services at St. Ninian's Cathedral, Perth. The Royal Family was staunch Presbyterian. When the Royal Family would walk into church, the congregants arose, recognizing their stature. They would remain standing while the Royal Family walked down the aisle to their pews. Then the minister came in to start the service.

Even as a teen, Lady Elizabeth was such a gracious lady. She had the most beautiful smile and she smiled at all present. She was such a beautiful girl and everyone loved her.

There was a tradition in St. Ninian's, and I think it is lovely. The rich girls were grouped in a Sunday School class after church; they were called the Sunshine Girls. Every year each girl would adopt a poor child from the church and they would be unknown to the chosen girl. The Sunshine Girls would find out the chosen girls' birthdays and give them a gift. On every special occasion, these children would receive something from their Sunshine Girl. They never knew who their benefactor was until Christmas, and then it was divulged.

One year, Lady Elizabeth was my mother's Sunshine Girl. My mother was most excited to find out Lady Elizabeth was her benefactor. She gave Mother a lovely white lace handkerchief and a pair of beautiful, white kidskin gloves. Mother had a little treasure box for these things, which disappeared when she left Scotland to marry my father. She left it behind, then when she wrote back and asked for it, nobody knew what happened to it. She never used the gloves or handkerchief; they were such a luxury for her, special to wear. Mother said, "I didn't make a fuss about them. It was over and done with. But they were the only things I ever valued as a child."

Long after my mother's father, Donald MacPhee, went back to India without seeing his newborn daughter, another Donald MacPhee, came into her life. This Donald MacPhee was her father's uncle, and played the bagpipes for the Queen Mother when she was in Balmoral Castle, Scotland.

He was in the musical part of the army. He was Lady Elizabeth's favorite piper. Alarm clocks were not popular and Lady Elizabeth didn't like being awakened by the footman. So the piper would stand under her windows and play "Scotland, the Brave" or one of her other favorite Scottish numbers to awaken her.

Lady Elizabeth Bowes-Lyon, who was Lilian's Sunshine Girl at St. Ninians' church in Perth, is pictured above as a teen. Lady Elizabeth became Queen Elizabeth after her husband, Prince Albert, ascended to the throne. She was the mother of the current reigning monarch of Britain, Queen Elizabeth II.

On Sundays they used to have programs in the church. They found my mother had a beautiful singing voice. If she'd been trained, she could have been an opera singer. It is a pity she wasn't. She sang in the choir. In England and Scotland, sometimes children dance the local folkloric dances in church. Donald MacPhee saw my mother dance and saw that she was a good dancer. He asked if she'd like dance lessons. Her granny let her take dancing lessons, much to Mother's surprise. He taught her for free because she was a relative and he knew that she could not pay for the lessons. But my mother didn't know they were related and her father was never mentioned. Donald MacPhee started teaching her when she was about 11. She held the Scottish dancing championship for two or three years in a row when she was only about 13 or 14, which was unheard of.

In those days, they finished school at about 13 or 14 years of age. As she got into her late teens, Mother was dancing and she was working at the railroad station. Her Uncle George Burns, Aunt Rose's husband, was under-manager and later station manager for Glasgow Central Railroad Station.

They used to have kiosks near the platforms where they'd sell ice cream, cigarettes, cigars, chewing gum, and candy bars, all kinds of stuff. Young women would wear small celluloid trays that hung around their necks and sell these items to passengers on incoming trains.

Prince Edward, who abdicated the throne prior to marrying Wallis Simpson, often passed through the station and he would always buy cigarettes from my mother; he always gave her a nice tip. She met Winston Churchill one time at the station and he bought something from her, I'm not sure what, we think possibly one of his iconic cigars. She also met the real King George, Edward's father.

Glasgow Station is where she met my father, John Carter Burchell. He was from Watford, Hertfordshire, about 17 miles north of London. He was working as a dining car attendant on the Flying Scotsman, the train that connected London and Scotland.

Mother was lovely, an attractive ginger blonde and blue-eyed, with very nice features and she caught his eye. She was 17 and he was seven years older. This was probably her one and only boyfriend; I don't recall ever hearing her talk about other boyfriends.

They ran away together. I think she left and just didn't tell anybody, because there was such hostility over it from her family. She was excommunicated from the family for a long time because she left and because he was English, not welcomed into a Scottish family. It was a long time until Mother saw her family again.

My mother and her soon-to-be husband probably just

arranged to meet at the train station. I don't know where they got married, England or Scotland, or whether they were married first, then ran away. Mother felt that was all very private. My feeling is that they must have been attracted to each other and just ran away, because the marriage was not deeply thought out. They knew so little about each other before marriage.

I think they moved to Hornchurch immediately, but I don't know what brought them there. It doesn't make a lot of sense. He was from Watford. Hornchurch was on the train line, but not the train on which he worked. So my father had to travel 35 miles to get to his job on the Flying Scotsman.

The Flying Scotsman began operating between Edinburg, Scotland, and London, England, in 1923, a route that had been in existence since 1862. The British Empire Exhibition in 1924-25 made the train famous. In 1928, a new type of tender made it possible for a replacement driver and fireman to take over at the halfway point without stopping. The 1928 non-stop Flying Scotsman also had improved catering and other on-board services, even a barber's shop. The Flying Scotsman was retired in 1963. Since 2006, the National Railway Museum has had the train in restoration to become a working museum exhibit. When it returns to the tracks, it will be the oldest working mainline locomotive in Britain and has been deemed a national treasure. - flyingscotsman.org.uk

The marriage was disastrous. I remember that my mother hated his smoking, but he was a smoker when she married him. Maybe she thought she would break him of it, but no. He was a scoundrel, a drinker, but not a drunk or a gambler. Most people in England drink more than I think they should. Mother's own grandmother had breast cancer and they had to lop off her breast and in those days they had to take out all the nerves under the arm. She was in terrible, terrible pain. She'd never been a drinker, frowned upon alcohol in the house, but after her surgery, she took to drinking gin. My mother didn't know whether the gin killed her or the cancer. She would be much calmer when she drank and the pain was less.

At first, I don't think Mother knew about my father's other women. He'd spend one night on the train and if he was away more than one night, there might have been a suspicion. When she found out that he had had several affairs, she kicked him out of our home. At first he supported us, but after they were separated, not at all.

Everybody wanted to know why she married that rascal; she could have had anybody. I really don't know much about my father. It wasn't just that my mother wouldn't talk about him; I don't have even one photograph of him, only memories. She said he was no good and destroyed all his pictures.

They were married 13 years and she had five girls to him. He died at about age 40 of double pneumonia; I was around five.

Lilian MacPhee Burchell is pictured above in her early 20s. It was around this time that Jasmine was born.

PART I: A CHILD IN WAR-TORN ENGLAND

Chapter 2

I was born May 7, 1934, in Oldchurch Hospital, Romford, Essex. My birth certificate states Hornchurch, but I was actually born in the hospital at Romford. Hornchurch was my home.

I was christened at Hornchurch Church, which was the Episcopal church, at about eight months of age, I imagine, although I don't, of course, remember that. We did have a certificate, but by the end of the war we had lost a lot of stuff. We did have a lot of bombings and paper didn't fare well when the slats were shaken off the roof and rain came in.

Jasmine was Lilian's biggest baby at almost 12 pounds. She was always told she won baby pageants because of her appearance as a "healthy," bouncing baby girl.

I weighed 12 pounds when I was born—well, one ounce off 12 pounds. I won all the baby competitions. People said, "That kid's not three months old, that kid's not six months old, that's a full-grown kid." Beautiful? No, I won because I was so big. They chose me because I looked so healthy. I had good skin. I was a nice healthy baby, a big, bouncy baby. I was Mother's biggest baby, the third daughter. Mother ended up having five daughters, two of which did not survive childhood.

Phyllis Helen Merrit was the oldest. She hated the name Phyllis, so we always called her Helen. I don't know how Mother came up with her name. Helen grew up to be really pretty: short, 5 feet 1, maybe shorter. She had wonderful legs and pretty feet, red hair. It was a natural auburn, curly. Everybody envied her hair. She didn't have the skin of a red-head, more like a blonde. She had hazel eyes that were usually green. She was very attractive and petite. She won a scholarship to the Royal Academy of Dramatic Arts in London. She married Lawrence "Laurie" Beavis, an English Army officer, who fought and was wounded in the Korean conflict. Laurie was a newspaper man and they eventually moved to St. Thomas, Ontario, Canada. Helen worked in Canadian television quite a lot and also repertory theater in Canada. She loved the theater and was a good actress. She enjoyed comedy roles as well. She and Laurie had three children, Allison, Bruce, and Jennifer. Helen died in 2013 in her 80s.

Mother carried her second daughter, Destiny, to term but she died at birth. I was third, then came Melody, who died of pneumonia in childhood.

Lilian, Jasmine and Helen celebrate a birthday in party hats. Jasmine is the child in arms while little Helen shows off her splits.

I am Jasmine Dolores Careen, pronounced Karen, (my mother used to read a lot). Jasmine is Mediterranean, Dolores is Spanish, and Careen is Russian. Throughout my childhood, I was a very ordinary-looking child. After being so big as a baby, I grew into a skinny kid, with straight mousy blonde hair that had streaks of gold running through it. I had large freckles so they nicknamed me "Freckle Face." I prayed for the freckles to fade and they finally did as I grew older. Someone told me to use real cream from a cow to fade freckles and I always begged for the cream when anyone had milk, and I smeared it all over my face. It was good for my skin but did nothing for my freckles.

I was a busy kid, involved in everything and I loved to run. I rode my bike and climbed trees. I drove my mother crazy tearing up my knees. Because the only girls in our neighborhood were older and didn't want to play with me, I had to play with the boys. We loved to play rounders, which was our version of baseball.

Davina Louise is the youngest of my mother's daughters and lives in Hilden, Germany, a small town very close to Düsseldorf. Davina is an old Scottish family name, it goes back a long way. It means "beloved." As a baby, Davina was also very sickly and we nearly lost her, too. When she started growing, from about seven on, she was so cute and sweet; she made friends easily. She was well-liked at school. Davina had beautiful skin. She was blonde and blue-eyed. When she started ballet, her figure started changing. She was attractive and still is. My folks moved to Toronto, Canada, when Davina was a teenager. That became her home. She was fortunate to join the Royal Canadian Ballet Company and danced and traveled with them for a number of years.

She met her husband, Edmond Skedzuhn, a German, who was studying in Canada. They married and he worked in Canada for a number of years before they moved to Germany permanently. We tried to trace where our two little sisters, Destiny and Melody, were buried, but even now we can't find their graves. I've been back to the church several times and asked the deacons. Surely somebody made a note where these bodies were buried. I tried to visit their graves but they were unmarked because they were not christened in the church and therefore not allowed in the formal church graveyard. They had to be buried in unconsecrated ground. Strange times, those were. Mother fought with the church over it, but that's the way it was.

Hornchurch was a sleepy little village until the war years. It was spread out over a good-sized area. The school system was good. There were paved streets and sidewalks. It became an important place because of the aerodrome after the war started.

My parents bought the bungalow at 194 Suttons Avenue on the "never-never," meaning it takes a long time to pay off. That's where we lived when I was born. Because it was nearly new, I think they probably bought it from the builder. My mother named the house "Jasmine Dene." I don't know if it still goes by the same name now or not. Suttons Avenue was a major street running through Hornchurch; we lived near where it ended in a rural area. It was a lovely little house, white with pretty dark blue shutters and picket-style fence with a hand bell at the gate. Most of the homes were very uniform in appearance, rows of houses that looked alike. There were not many isolated cottages like ours, with concrete walls and floors. They had been built earlier.

I remember so clearly that there was a flu epidemic when I was four. I was sick. It was a nice warm day and I wanted to go to the garden to play. My mother said I couldn't because I might spread the flu. We had to maintain ourselves inside. We could color, read books, listen to the radio. The city could fine us if we didn't stay inside. They didn't want to spread the flu around. The visitors who came wore masks, hats, and gloves. People delivered our groceries to the front gate. They would ring the hand bell and we had to wait until they left to go out and pick up our food. We were quarantined in our home.

When I was not quite five, my father came home from work with a very bad cold which turned into the flu. He gave it to our family. I believe this was about 1938. My younger sister Melody, my father, and I all went to the hospital when it turned into pneumonia. Then it turned into double pneumonia and breathing became labored. We were mighty sick.

I remember being in the hospital. I got scarlet fever in addition to pneumonia and my lung collapsed. Then I got scabies, which was open sores. They tied my hands to the bars to prevent me scratching them. Ever since then, I have had a fear of having my hands under the covers.

I remember the terrible itch of the scabies. I was tearing myself to pieces. Changing the dressings was often very painful. When the sores got dry, they stuck to the dressings and there was one nurse who would just rip the dressing off. I remember the pain and her telling me, when I would cry, to stop being a baby. I remember the antiseptic smells. And I remember the delicious smell from the dinner trays. I was usually hungry despite all else.

I wasn't in a ward; I was contagious and coughing. It seemed like I was there for an eternity, but everything does to a child. Maybe I was there two or three months. Everything was starched and uncomfortable: sheets, pillowcases, the nurses' uniforms were very scratchy with starched hats. Everything was so white and there were metal bars around the bed like a crib. It was all so sterile, but I don't remember nurses and visitors wearing masks.

Mother did not get the flu. She could not visit us; she was pregnant with Davina, her fifth child. She came as often as she could, but she was only able to see me through a window and I was unable to see her. I was unaware that she was there half the time. She stopped by every day, but I don't remember seeing her more than once or twice. I remember feeling unhappy and alone and thinking I must look awful.

My younger sister Melody died in the hospital. When it was time for me to leave to go home, my mother questioned the nurse because I was so pale and skinny from my ordeal. Mother said, "This is not my child." But my baby footprint, taken at the hospital when I was born, proved I was indeed Jasmine. So home I went with my mother to be loved and nurtured and free again.

My father got out of the hospital during that time and went to live with his mother in Watford. He and my mother separated once and for all. We never saw him again.

Mother delivered Davina on August 28, 1939, after a difficult pregnancy and several periods of hemorrhaging. It was about one month before England declared war on Germany.

When my father died, we were in a lot of debt. Although they had been separated at the time of his death, Mother got a daytime job and worked hard to pay off his debts, as well as to make a life for us.

She worked for a Mrs. Newell who had a small business selling knickknacks—buttons, zippers, needles, thread, etc—in the downstairs of her home. She hired my mom from Monday through Saturday to run the shop, as she had a very sick husband to care for. The shop was in downtown Hornchurch about a mile from our home.

There were plenty of times I don't think we would have made it if my mother, a single mother with three children, hadn't gone to the Salvation Army and told them she couldn't pay the bills. They always came through. I still support them to this day.

Mother was beautiful, about five feet two inches, slender, big busted. She started out with mousy brown hair and went blonde.

In a family portrait, Jasmine's sisters, Helen and Davina, are pictured with mom Lilian.

When you do it yourself, it's not the same color every week, but she was always very attractive. She dressed well for our conditions. She hired a lady who made clothes. Mother would buy material, take to the lady, and she would make a skirt or blouse and charge only a little. She was envied by a lot of women, whose husbands did a double take when they saw her. But she wasn't looking for a man. She was just trying to keep her head above water, be true to herself, and keep us safe.

As I have said, Mother had a good singing voice so she took a second job, singing at the aerodrome dances; they would pay her a few shillings almost every Saturday night. Hours at Mrs. Newell's were long and busy, but sometimes she would stop by on her way home to sing a couple of Scottish songs to the new recruits for a half hour or so. Helen stayed home with us and did her homework. Sometimes a woman in charge of the cafeteria at the aerodrome gave Mother sandwiches to bring home. Everybody was so kind.

On Sundays about once a month, Mother had to go to market in London to buy yarn, buttons, etc., merchandise for Mrs. Newell's knickknack store. Mother would sometimes let me go, too. The man who owned the warehouse, a Jewish man named Sid, would order in sandwiches: corned beef, salami, bologna, sometimes a little roast beef—always meat—which wasn't available to everybody because of the rationing. The sandwiches were two to three inches thick. Then he would pack a bunch of sandwiches for us to take home.

The sandwiches always came with dill pickles, which I absolutely loathed. Mother said, "I'm going to watch you, don't say a word. You realize Sid is on rations too." I'd try to swallow whatever it was that I didn't like when Mother was watching, but it was difficult. I would throw out pieces when Mother wasn't watching. I never liked dill pickles, and still don't today. She'd wrap the pickles in anything that wasn't being used, put them in her purse and carry them home; she wouldn't even let me leave them there. The smell...even at that age, a pickle wasn't something I enjoyed smelling. Mother would say, "Eat it, it won't kill you." I really wondered if she was right.

Part of the time, Sid's daughter, Sophie, worked in the warehouse. She gave me buttons. There was a machine you could use to cover the button with material. The buttons were in two separate pieces and you'd pull the handle down to push the upper part into the lower part. I loved to play with that. I made all kinds of buttons and they let me take them home and put them on my dolly's clothes. And I had a

Jasmine's mother, Lilian MacPhee Burchell, was married to Jasmine's father for only about 13 years. This photo was taken about the time she struck out on her own with three small children.

beautiful blouse with buttons to match. Sophie showed me how to do a little embroidery. They had a tatting machine and I loved to play with the lace. She gave me all kinds of sparkly things. If they'd make up something for a customer, she might give me little pieces of it for my doll's collar. She was so kind to me.

Despite my mother's working two jobs, money was still very tight. There was a widows' pension you could get if you were without aid from your husband or he was ill and couldn't work. You had to jump through hoops, like now with the welfare system here; you had to meet certain standards. One of them was that you couldn't own property. We had been buying the house we lived in but Mother had to sell the house and apply for the widows' pension. We had to move out and leave our beloved home to strangers.

My mother was a proud woman. For her to ask for a widows' pension was one of the hardest things she ever had to do in her life. And it was still barely enough to keep us alive.

So, when I was about six, we moved into a council house, which means the rent was subsidized by the government, on Winkletye Lane. I don't remember the number, but it was near the church. It was in a row of two-story houses. There was no basement. The council houses were for people who had had sad times and needed help, and we did.

Out the back door was a covered porch and next to that was our coal cellar and the door to the toilet. There was always a debate over whether you wanted to use the chamber pot in your bedroom or go downstairs and out the door in the cold air to the toilet. You had to cross a small outdoor space and there was no heat in the toilet. If there was wind, you really didn't want to go out there, especially at night.

Our previous cottage had had a proper bathroom with running water. We realized that we had lost stature when we moved. The house had very little privacy, but if your financial situation was bad, you did what you had to. There was a lot of humiliation that came with moving to a council house.

The house had a big round tub, kind of like a barrel. It was quite deep, I'd say about four feet deep. We ran water from the kitchen sink via a long hose to the tub and heat the water over a burner underneath for a bath or laundry. Or there was a four-legged tub with a cold water tap adjacent to it. You could do laundry there or take a bath. You had to be small to sit in it. Adults could wash up to their belly button, but most of the time people just went to the public shower houses in town if they wanted to wash their hair or anything more than their armpits.

People then were so proud of their homes, even if they were council houses. Everyone had polished brass door knockers. There were no doorbells. We polished the knockers every day. We thoroughly swept our porches. The metal pieces that ran under the doorway had to shine like the sun. We cleaned them with Brasso. We might be poor, but we were always so clean and tidy. No matter whether you were poor or not, you could still ask the Queen Mum in for tea. And she did come into people's homes on occasion. After a bombing, she would stop by some of the homes and say, "Oh my, what a terrible time you've had." And they'd ask if she would like to come in for tea and she would say, "I'd love to." She would cry along with them over the loss of their cherished belongings. She was also so gracious and kind and loved by all for her unpretentiousness.

Our house was whitewashed about once a year and it was up to the council to keep it up. The houses actually joined at the roof line. There was a thick privet hedge growing around the houses and on the other side of the hedge was a metal fence. On your side of the hedge, you could grow flowers. We had lilac bushes, one white and one purple, in our backyard. The smell was heavenly.

Everybody loved flowers. No matter how poor you were, there were always flower beds, flower boxes, or flowering trees; it didn't matter if it was just daffodils. And there was a little part of the yard where you could grow vegetables, especially during the war years.

Mother usually had a half day off on Thursday. She would do a lot of cooking that day. She baked tarts and pies and made stews. She would have the windows up on a hot day and you would know by the smells if she was making jelly or jam or if there was an apple pie. I was always happy going home from school on Thursdays. You could smell the aromas emitting from our house all the way from the road. It's funny what you remember. There were wonderful smells, food that would out-smell the flowers in the garden.

We lived in three houses in Hornchurch, the bungalow and two council houses. The third house was at 28 Prior's Park. It was closer to the airport. I believe we moved to the second council house because of structural damage to the first, or maybe we had just outgrown the house on Winkletye Lane.

As poor as we were, Mother was always generous. A shilling, which is 12 cents, was like about $10 today—a lot to us. But Mother would give away three shillings every Christmas—one to the dustman, or garbage man as Americans would call him, one to the guy who delivered coal to our house, and one to the chimney sweep. It was unusual for people in our position. But Mother always said they did their jobs and deserved a proper recompense.

My mother would buy what she could afford at Christmastime. We didn't gift wrap then, but put it in a brown paper bag and that's how you got your Christmas present. But she couldn't stand to have things not given. Two or three days before Christmas she would say, "I think you should have one of your gifts right now." I hated this. I like to think of what I might get. I've been that way all my life. I like the anticipation of the gift as much as the opening. The imagining was the most important part. She would give us hints. I'd think, "It's soft and cuddly. It must be a teddy bear." I would wonder what color my teddy bear was. Did it have button eyes? Shiny eyes? A big smile?

When we could find one, we'd have a Christmas tree. When the lot was nearly empty, they would sell them cheaply. But a tree was not as important as the big, long stocking on the mantle. Mother would stuff them with fruit and candy. Our gift was usually a new sweater or jacket or shoes or maybe gloves or socks. It was what you needed, not what you wanted. Everything was rationed. If you had a bar of chocolate among the fruit, really it was the best present, a whole bar to yourself. Today a kid would throw it on the floor. But we treasured everything.

My mother was not only generous, but brave, kind, and loyal. She was very loving, but not demonstrative. She didn't know how to say she loved us. There was no hugging or kissing. Mother never showed great, deep affection. I think she just wasn't brought up with much display of affection. I don't remember ever seeing my father hold her hand or kiss her.

Although she didn't show a lot of affection, it was clear that Mother was very proud of us. She would give us the Giaconda smile, that's Italian for Mona Lisa, when she was pleased. She had great ambitions for us all. She wanted us to rise above the situation; if we didn't do it on our own, she was behind us pushing. We made the grade, no matter what it was.

PART I: A CHILD IN WAR-TORN ENGLAND

Chapter 3

In England, you started school at a much earlier age. But I had pneumonia so I missed the deadline to enter school. I was about a half year behind everybody else. The rest of the class had been in school half a year, learning the alphabet. The teacher tried hard to catch me up. But nobody realized, including me, that, in addition to being behind, I was also dyslexic. My major problems were recognizing words and numbers.

I finally managed to conquer the words when things were written down. We didn't have a lot of books, but things were written on the blackboard and we transposed them to paper. In the time of taking my eyes from the blackboard, I was no longer sure what I'd seen so I had to guess. I had great difficulties with numbers in particular. Words that were in books were easier; I could close my eyes and try to remember what I'd seen. I learned speed reading at an early age, by reading fast and leaving out all the small words, like "to," "it," and "for." I'd close my eyes and remember what I'd seen, and I could come up with a sentence that made sense. Thank the Lord, it worked.

It took a lot longer to conquer not knowing left and right. That caused me problems on the playground. We were supposed to

Jasmine, front right, joins her first grade class for a class photo. She soon found she had dyslexia and a beautiful singing voice.

line up and then march left, right, left, right, but I didn't know what was left and what was right. That did not make the teachers happy. I finally conquered it by wearing a rubber band on my left wrist. Then I could start with the foot on the same side as the rubber band. There were some really odd things, some whacko things about me. We couldn't afford a wristwatch or a bracelet, but you could get rubber bands all over the place. I kept it there all the time, it was my constant companion. It was years before I could take the rubber band off.

I was short for my age—a large baby, but small build, not tall as I grew. When we'd go to school, we had prayers first, then went into the gymnasium where we spent 30 minutes doing all kinds of things. The children were expected to vault over a horse; well, it looks like a horse and the children put their hands on it and vaulted over it. I watched all the children before it was my turn. I thought, "I'm going to run right into that and go splat." I was running toward it with dread in my heart. But somehow it all came together. I was so proud. I wanted everybody to applaud but they didn't.

PART I: A CHILD IN WAR-TOWN ENGLAND

Chapter 4

Hornchurch had been a very peaceful town until the war, probably considered more like a village. It had the only airport between London and the coast. It was where young people trained to fly. At first it was not an Air Force base, it did not belong to the government. Anybody who had the money could learn to fly. But later it became a base for war planes.

Spitfires rally at Royal Air Force Hornchurch, minutes from Jasmine's house, in 1940. That same year the one-man fighter planes and Hornchurch's airfield played a major role in the Battle of Britain and the Dunkirk evacuation. *Photo courtesy Brooks Aviation Art.*

Hornchurch Airfield became Royal Air Force Hornchurch during World War II. It was originally opened as an airstrip on Sutton's Farm in 1915, where biplanes soon defended London in World War I. At the end of the war, the airfield returned to agriculture, but it became an airfield again before World War II, when it was a Sector Airfield in 11 Group Fighter Command. Three squadrons were stationed there and equipped with Spitfires, a one-man fighter plane. The airfield played a major role during the Dunkirk evacuation in 1940 and the Battle of Britain. It was bombed on 20 occasions. – pastscape.org.uk

When suddenly England declared war on Germany in 1939, it was a very frightening period. Much of it I didn't understand at the time; I was only five years old. Adolf Hitler already had marched his soldiers into Poland, and it already had been taken. England declared that if Germany took over Poland, we would declare war. They had their machinery all ready for action and we, the British, had very little. We were scrambling to get things together and get everybody prepared. All the young men were called out to service. We would see them marching and training.

On September 3, 1939, British Prime Minister Neville Chamberlain declared war on Germany. He was joined by France, Australia and New Zealand. The following May, Winston Churchill became the new prime minister. Two days later, the German army entered France. On May 14, the Local Defense Volunteers ("Dad's Army") was created. It was later called the Home Guard. In June, German troops took over the Channel Islands, between France and England, the only British soil ever occupied by Germany. France surrendered to Germany on June 22. The Battle of Britain, the campaign by the German Air Force to take over Britain, began July 10, 1940.
– www.britannica.com

There have been a lot of traumatic moments in my life. War, hearing the words uttered that "we are at war," that was a terrible moment. It chilled me. Remember I was only five years old. We were listening to Prime Minister Neville Chamberlain on the radio. You could have heard a pin drop, and then my mother

Newspapers worldwide announced Britain's war with Germany on September 4, 1939. Among Jasmine's historic collections is a re-creation of that day's tabloid newspaper, *The Daily Sketch.*

started crying. I knew it was something terrible. My mother was scared, so I was scared. Mother knew what was coming. She had been through the 1914 war, World War I.

That was probably the most traumatic moment of my life. I kept asking Mother what war was and why did people do it. Why would people want to kill other people? I can't remember her answer now, but I knew we were in a vulnerable place.

Our little aerodrome mushroomed overnight to become a strategic air base. Those little two-winged planes, known as biplanes, were replaced by things we hadn't seen before. The Spitfire was one of them, a one-seater with just the pilot. He maneuvered the guns as well as the action of the plane; it was a very maneuverable plane. The pilot had to get out of some very tight places.

Two men from the local defense office came around and rang our door bell and asked my mother, "Would you donate your chain fence to the war effort? We need all the metal we can get." She said, "If it's for the war, take it away. It's one of those things we can do without." And then people came around at the school and gave us gas masks and said we had to learn to use them. "We don't know if they'll use the gas like in the first war," they said, referring to the mustard gas. "But we may have to use the gas masks." So that was the beginning.

We had "blackout" enforced in our homes so the Germans couldn't spot targets when they bombed at night. We'd place a piece of wood in the window to hold the blackout shades tight. We were told there could be no light showing through when we turned on the lights, to keep planes from identifying any target. They wanted a complete blackout. My older sister and I used to put the shades into place every night just before dark. Before the war, people didn't often have curtains or shades. I don't know how we lived without them. Usually there were just little lacy curtains across the top and nothing else.

Lights would not be allowed after dark for almost six years, and some said the blackout became the most unpopular aspect of the war for civilians, more than rationing. By the time you got home from school and had supper, it was already dark. The dark is not a pleasant place to be when you are doing homework or washing your hair. You couldn't write letters. We'd try to write by candlelight, but the candles would flicker, making it difficult. You felt inadequate to do the things you normally do.

The most awful part was people screaming in the dark, then the devastation left behind when a bomb went off. It was very scary, the not knowing what damage had been done, what you would find when you went out.

People in London didn't have air raid shelters, so they went to the train stations. There was no way to build a large bomb shelter in the short period of time that we had to prepare. At first, people used their basements as shelter, but not everyone had a basement. And then when a house was hit, the bomb frequently imploded,

The Daily Sketch explained to British citizens what to do in case of an air raid. This re-creation is dated September 4, 1939.

and the people were stuck inside the basement, often suffocating before being found.

Then there was the Anderson shelter. It was outside the house, half buried with earth heaped on top, kind of like a root cellar, to protect from bomb blasts underground. Corrugated iron sheets were bolted together at the top, with steel plates at either end. The only problem was the moisture of the Essex soil. It would seep into the shelter over a period of time and we would get quite a bit of water in there. It was impossible to keep dry.

I met Julie Andrews years ago. She gave this talk about the war years in London. She couldn't remember the name of the shelters outside of the house. Afterwards I spoke to her and told her they were called Anderson shelters. She laughed and said, "Well, you were obviously around." I said, "Yes, and we had an Anderson shelter which we used whenever possible."

One night the bombing was very intense all around us. We ran to the outdoor shelter and I was first in line. Mother gave me a little push to hurry me up. I fell into a lot of water. So she said, "Okay, the rest of you don't go down there." She asked, "Did you get very wet?" I was soaked and it was so cold. Mother ran and got a dry towel. Everybody was forever trying to keep water out of the shelter, but it was just the moisture from the soil. And, there would be tiny little spiders and newts in the shelter.

Almost everybody had victory gardens. We sustained ourselves the best way we could by growing anything and everything. Germany was trying to starve us out. We had depended on shipping for food so much. Our rations were two ounces of beef per person per week, two ounces of butter per person per week, two eggs, etc. There was no such thing as going out and buying 10 pounds of potatoes. It was minimal everything. We got one pair of shoes every six months and we purchased them too large and stuffed them with old newspaper to make them fit. This is why my feet are like this, it forced my big toe over my other toes. My feet are terrible. But everything was so highly rationed. My school hat was so big it kept falling off; my mother stuffed it with newspaper, too. We had an elastic strap under my chin to keep it on when the wind blew.

The ration card was issued to you and you had an identification card. All legal citizens had to keep the ration and identification cards with them at all times. When we were later evacuated, I was seven, I became responsible for my younger sister Davina's identification and rationing card. The oldest children were given the responsibility for the youngest, it was part of that time.

If we were trying to come to terms with our new life, so was our government. This was not just a war of speech, saying nasty things to each other. It was a war of planes and bombs. Suddenly we went into the 20th century where you had to exercise caution. We had been far too trusting in the past and now we had to realize the lesson of "kill" or "be killed." We grew up that way; suddenly it was a different kind of world. Hitler wanted to humble everybody. People were horrified to think that someone would go in and try to wipe out a whole city. That's the way we were, naive.

During the war, British citizens were allowed only two ounces of beef per person per week, two eggs and two ounces of butter. The only way to buy food was with a ration card.

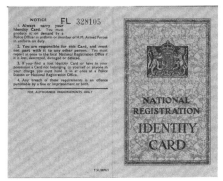

The British government required that a national registration card be carried by every citizen at all times during World War II. When evacuated at age seven with her two-year-old sister, Jasmine was responsible for not only her card but that of her sister.

There was absolutely no ethics in this war. And our Prime Minister Neville Chamberlain wasn't tough enough for those times.

Winston Churchill, thank God he was there. He became our new leader and boldly gave us strength. He wasn't just blowing off steam when he said, "We shall fight on the beaches, we shall fight on the landing grounds, we shall fight in the fields and in the streets, we shall fight in the hills." It was a wonderful speech. Suddenly enemy planes were dropping bombs everywhere. Our planes were not built to carry all those bombs. It was a very fearful time. We were learning as we were going. We were fighting with so little, but we learned quickly.

Churchill never lied to us. He came on broadcast TV and told us we might be undermanned, but we would not be underplayed.

Churchill to the House of Commons, June 4, 1940: "We shall go on to the end, we shall fight in France, we shall fight on the seas and oceans, we shall fight with growing confidence and growing strength in the air, we shall defend our Island, whatever the cost may be, we shall fight on the beaches, we shall fight on the landing grounds, we shall fight in the fields and in the streets, we shall fight in the hills; we shall never surrender, and even if, which I do not for a moment believe, this Island or a large part of it were subjugated and starving, then our Empire beyond the seas, armed and guarded by the British Fleet, would carry on the struggle, until, in God's good time, the New World, with all its power and might, steps forth to the rescue and the liberation of the old." - winstonchurchill.org

Hornchurch was approximately 35 miles, maybe a little farther, east of London. When they came, Hitler's air force swarmed across Hornchurch like a black cloud, hundreds of planes in the sky all at once, all flying low, loaded as they were with bombs, although I didn't know that at the time. I was five-and-a-half-years old, I hadn't been evacuated at that time; in fact, the worst was nearly over by the time we were evacuated. I remember being on the playground when the teachers began screaming and running and trying to get us all together. They were all looking up and telling us to run, not to look up.

I can't remember what teacher it was, screaming, "Go in there right now." We were all so amazed, we just stood there. We were overwhelmed by the enormous number of planes. "I'm going to put you all on report, all of you standing there. You're going to do extra homework," she was screaming. She would have been a week getting all the names down. There were bombs overhead and they could start shooting at any moment. We didn't know if the pilot might press the button and start shooting by accident or even use us as target practice.

We finally ran into the gym. We knew things were bad but nothing happened to us—we were safe.

During the London Blitz, the planes went over us in Hornchurch. It was like a bunch of birds coming and coming and coming. I don't remember seeing them come back over; maybe we were in the shelter. Then, once England got the Spitfires up and ready, we were right in the middle of the action. The Spitfires were located at Hornchurch and took to the air from there for the dogfights. The German plane was a Messerschmitt. Ours was a much smaller plane. The beauty was that the bigger planes couldn't get out of the way of ours. The skill of the Spitfire pilots kept us alive. It was like a hummingbird coming up under a goose and attacking it from the front. I doubt England would be the same today if not for the Spitfire.

I remember seeing them do it. The Spitfires would fly up as soon as they saw planes flying to London. They would keep under their bellies and come up in front of the pilot, turn and fire on them, then drop back down. It was a work of art the way they did it. Rows and rows of bullets ran through their guns as fast as they could. Rolls Royce built those engines, they were fantastic. Terrific speed. They danced around in front of the Messerschmitts, which couldn't avoid them because they are big lumbering planes. Then the Spitfire had to get out of the way because, having killed the pilot, the plane was coming down. The Spitfire had to drop away quickly because the German plane, which was full of bombs, would explode.

At around 4 p.m. September 7, 1940, a swarm of 348 German bombers, escorted by 617 fighters, blackened the London skies. Bombs fell until 7 p.m. Two hours later, a second group of raiders arrived with another attack that lasted until 4:30 a.m. Coming to be known as the London Blitz, or Blitzkrieg in German, the bombing continued until the following May. Over a period of 267 days, London was attacked 71 times.

In the first weeks of the Blitz, there were not enough shelters, so many residents ran to the Underground station. Later, other surface and underground shelters were implemented as community shelters and private shelters were built by homes. In the worst single incident, 450 people were killed when a bomb destroyed a school being used as an air raid shelter. Over the course of the Blitz, more than one million London houses were destroyed or damaged, and more than 40,000 civilians were killed, almost half of them in London. The Blitz ended on May 11, 1941.
– www. eyewitnesstohistory.com

The earlier bombs dropped by the Germans were incendiary bombs—devices designed to start fires—made of either magnesium and iron powders or of petroleum. When they would hit the target, their weight and fire would make them burn their way through the ceiling. Most ceilings were made of wood and then rubber tile or whatever, but they were not a solid surface. The bottom floor, often the basement, was made of concrete. The bombs burned their way through the roof and dropped to the next floors. It would burn until it hit the concrete; that's when it exploded.

We were so close to the aerodrome, the planes either flew directly over our school or partially over it, both coming and going to London. We children were aware of everything. Hornchurch was under the gun. We were among the early ones to get bombed. It was constant, night and day. They were trying to make us give in, bend our knees and give in, make us capitulate, but it didn't work. It just made us stronger and angrier.

Hornchurch was the first line of defense. If we hadn't caught the enemy planes and taken them out of action, they would be down on the coast. We had to try to stop them on their journey to London. If a German plane landed safely or if they could repair it, there would be one more German war plane that they could use in the fighting. I had thoughts in the back of my mind that if that pilot didn't bring the plane home, it would be one less to fight. If he went down, it would be another body no longer fighting. We kids would cheer like the devil when we saw them shoot down a German plane. It meant one less German to fight, a horrible man trying to kill us. It never became mundane. But if we saw one of our planes falling, we watched hopefully for a parachute. We knew we needed every man we had. And when an English parachute would open, we would all cheer that the pilot was safe.

You lost young men to the war, so the Home Guard was usually men my husband's age—sixties, seventies, even eighties. We had doctors, dentists, and all kinds of people in the Home Guard, everybody who could walk and help. A Home Guard volunteer stood on the roofs at night with binoculars around his neck, watching for planes coming in. He would call it in to the police department and the fire department who could then be planning their direction and preparing the towns ahead for their arrival.

We had about five big guns located around Hornchurch, but I don't remember hearing them go off. When a German plane went down, people would go to where they came down and would take the pilots as prisoners.

If they were flying high, it would mean they were going on to London. The sirens—located at the fire department—would be prepared to sound so we would know whether the planes were passing on. You could hear the rumble in the dark, and you'd know the planes were going over. The Home Guard members would still call them in to the fire department just in case; sometimes they suddenly lowered really fast and start dropping bombs. They were trying to get our airport. Generally you paid attention when you heard the planes. You could tell if the danger was immediate because the siren would be longer, moaning an unearthly noise—"ooooo-eeeee." If it cut off at a certain period, then they were flying high. The people sounding the alarm would try not to get you out of bed to go to the shelters unnecessarily.

Anytime you see a movie about World War II, when they have these big maps, the name Hornchurch is featured quite prominently. They'd be moving some of the planes up toward Hornchurch or bringing some of the English planes to try to catch the Germans before they got to Hornchurch and the Somerset area. The Germans were coming in mass to wipe us out. So many of our homes were destroyed, as you can imagine. Nobody felt really safe. You never knew when the bombs would strike, on the way in to London or on the way back. The planes were loaded with only so much gasoline and when they were weighed down with bombs as they were, it was eating up the gasoline. They unloaded the bombs on London, but when ground fire was too strong, they'd turn back and discharge the bombs over us. They didn't want anything left in that plane when it returned home and they wanted to save gasoline to be able to reach their home destination.

I've been shot at on my way to school. I know exactly what it sounds like to be shot at. It's a strange sound as the bullets hit the ground. The bombers would come down from the skies and try to get rid of the bullets and shoot every moving thing—kids, animals, anything, or nothing—just to frighten us or for target practice.

We walked across a farmer's field on the way to school. At first he tried to stop us, but he finally gave up and let us go through. He couldn't grow anything there, so he might as well make a pathway and let the children cross. There was a style, stairs over a fence, we crossed. We were quite vulnerable from the air there. There were trees in some parts of the field, but not around that style.

On the way to school or back, there might be 40 or 50 or 60 kids all in that field at the same time. The pilots would see us and dive bomb, unload their bullets, running them through their machine guns.

It's one of the reasons I'm an anti-gun person. I'm a nut about guns and I don't care who knows it. I've witnessed what guns can do. I've heard the screams. I didn't always know whether the kid behind me was hit or not. I was running and I didn't stop to find out. Maybe he just fell off the fence or maybe he was just fearful.

As we walked away from school, after the big field, there was an enormous fire station before you got to Main Street. When we were being fired upon, firemen would run out towards us, grab a couple of kids under each arm, throw them in the air raid shelter, then run back and grab two more. You didn't always see the firemen, they just came out of nowhere. Sometimes they were running from another angle and you'd just see an arm come out of nowhere to grab you. After awhile you got used to being scooped up and dumped, but at first it was as scary as the bombings. It was a very frantic time and I remember it vividly.

When there had been a bombing, I would leave for school early so I could walk down Main Street and avoid the neighborhoods. The neighborhoods were where a lot of the houses might have been destroyed; sometimes you could hear people screaming. Everybody heard the screams. There was smoke from the houses, people running with stretchers, somebody pouring blood. It was not a sight one wanted to see.

It's why I feel so sorry for kids in Bosnia now; they are living this life. My mother knew we were living it then, and she was too. She was three-and-a-half miles away from us at work. She could hear the planes, too, and knew they were strafing and trying to get rid of ammunition before they went back to base. She was aware of what was going on. We lived in total fear of this.

You didn't only have to worry about the bombs, there was a danger from the planes as well. Planes were crashing all over the place; our own forces were shooting them down, too. Hornchurch was getting a lot of bombs; other places were getting a lot of planes shot up. There was always stuff falling from the sky.

We saw constant bombing and the carnage and destruction that was the result of the bombing. And when we went to the movies, we saw the news reels and knew what was happening to the Jews in Europe. We saw the death camps. RKO Pictures showed the dead bodies. We saw the children's arms with numbers on them. I would turn my head, but I still saw. And we knew that the rest of Europe was suffering from German occupation.

People don't realize how close the Germans were to us. From Dover to Calais is only 20 miles of open water. We wondered every night if, when we woke up, we'd see Germans in our streets.

PART I: A CHILD IN WAR-TORN ENGLAND

Chapter 5

In 1941, at least I believe, the British government decided, especially in and around our area, that they were losing too many children. The children were the future. The government was aware that the Germans were dropping bombs anywhere that might do a lot of "good" for them. So it was decided that if you were under the age of 12, you had to be evacuated. I must have been around seven.

So many strange things have happened in our family. The British government said if we had family members elsewhere, the children could be sent there instead of evacuated to strangers. Mother wrote to Aunt Rose in Glasgow, who Mother said had never been kind to her. She said Aunt Rose called her a bastard, even though Granny would scold her.

Mother swallowed her

Several attempts were made during World War II to evacuate British children under the age of 12. The evacuations, where children were removed from their families to a safe zone, were announced in national newspapers, such as a re-creation of *The Daily Sketch*.

pride when she realized we had to be taken from London because of the bombing and the danger of losing too many children. If we couldn't send the children away to family, we would have to be evacuated to strangers.

So my mother wrote to Rose and asked, "Will you take them in?" The reply came right back, almost by return mail. She said, "I can't have them, and I'm not sure I would like to have them. I just bought a new suite of furniture. You'll have to make other arrangements."

At the time it seemed awful, but looking back, I don't really blame her. She had already raised her children. Rose was older and a much more controlled person than I ever was. The thought of me and my little sister, she was not sure she wanted to take us on.

But Mother was very upset. She wrote back, saying, "You may be far away from the bombs, Rose, but you are not far from God's wrath." About three months later, Rose's daughter, Marjorie, died of appendicitis. My mother, who believed in curses, always felt responsible for Marjorie's death.

At first, the government was planning to take children from London to Canada. I was supposed to be on a ship that was sunk by a mine; it was one of the times that I was supposed to be somewhere when something horrible happened but some kind of "faerie" luck intervened.

I was sick and didn't go. I think we had an epidemic of some kind so I didn't get to be evacuated to Canada because I was sick. Maybe it was diphtheria. I remember having a sore throat.

My mother said, "I wouldn't let you go to Canada all by yourself." I'm not sure if I didn't go because I was sick or if my mother just didn't want us traveling alone.

The government authorities said, "We won't put them on this ship, but they will have to go on the next." But there wasn't a next one.

The Children's Overseas Reception Board (CORB) was a rescue effort by the British government. A total of 2,664 children were evacuated from England by the board during the critical period between July and September 1940.

Most of the children were sent to four countries: Canada 1,532 (in nine parties), Australia 577 (three parties), New Zealand 202 (two parties), and South Africa 353 (two parties). Some also came to the United States of America. In the first few months over 211,000 children were registered to be evacuated. A further 24,000 children were approved for the evacuation and over 1,000 volunteer escorts, including doctors and nurses, were signed up to accompany the children for their temporary exile, with plans to return them to their families when the war was over.

Within two weeks of each other, two ships carrying the "sea evacuees" were torpedoed by German U-boats. The first was the Holland America Line's SS *Volendam*, whose passengers included 320 children bound for Halifax and New York. The ship left Liverpool on August 29, 1940 in a convoy of 33 ships. The convoy included RMS *Rangitata*, carrying 113 evacuee children headed for Wellington, New Zealand. On August 30, 1940 at about 11 p.m., the convoy was attacked by U-60. The *Volendam* was damaged and passengers and crew abandoned ship. All 300 children and the crew, except for the ship's purser, who was drowned, were rescued by other ships in the convoy and taken to Greenock, Scotland. The *Volendam* did not sink, and was towed to Scotland for repairs. A second unexploded torpedo was found in the bow; if it had exploded the ship would probably have sunk.

A second incident led to the cancellation of the CORB program. On September 17, 1940, the evacuation ship SS *City of Benares* (Ellerman Lines) was torpedoed and sunk, killing 77 of the 90 CORB children on board. The ship had left Liverpool on September 13, 1940, for Canada. The convoy of 20 ships, with the *City of Benares* in the lead, was 253 miles west-southwest of Rockall. At around 11:45 p.m. she was attacked by U-48. The first two torpedoes missed, but a second attack just after midnight hit the ship. She was abandoned and sank within 30 minutes. The British destroyer HMS *Hurricane* picked up 105 survivors and landed them at Greenock. Forty-two survivors were left adrift in a lifeboat for eight days, until being picked up by HMS *Anthony*. In addition to the children, the ship's master, the commodore, three staff members, 121 crew members and 134 passengers were lost. — www.johndreid.com

There were radio reports and pamphlets all over saying that Britain was evacuating children out of London on a cargo ship with red crosses on a white field, it couldn't be missed. And the Germans torpedoed it out of the water.

Things like this have happened to me several times in my life—times when I was supposed to be somewhere but wasn't. Mom said God gave us a power that we didn't understand. She said one day it would happen to me and I'd know. When I was about 12 and in the show *Cinderella*, I was supposed to take part in a promotional appearance

Royal Navy destroyer HMS *Anthony* rescues survivors from a lifeboat of the SS *City of Benares*. The ship carried children evacuated from their homes within the bombing area near London. The lifeboat had been adrift for nine days after the ship sank on September 17, 1940.

riding in a coach with two Shetland ponies. We were supposed to ride through town to the theater. That morning I woke up with a slight sore throat and I mentioned it to the promoter who had set things up. I told him I didn't feel good. He said, "You don't want to go on the coach?" I said, "I don't think so." So he got a chorus girl to dress as Cinderella and ride in the carriage. The horses ran away and the coach was dragged for a half block. The girl was badly injured. They never took the carriage out again.

Although I think this was my mother's unusual ability to see the future, I didn't actually see anything. I was just fearful about going in the coach. From then on when I had feelings about things, I paid attention. I was aware that I was developing my mother's ability.

Much later, there was a very bad train crash, one of the worst train crashes in England, on the same line my father traveled on. I missed it by 15 seconds. That should tell me something. My friend, Annette Bretton-Smith, and I were going to visit my aunt in Scotland. I must have been about 13 or 14 at that time. Annette was a lovely girl. I've often wondered what happened to her. We haven't been in touch in many years. She was a school friend who attended Italia Conti theatrical school when I did.

I was traveling into London on the electric underground train. There was a fire in the train tunnel so we all had to get off and walk to the nearest station, maybe a 10-minute walk. They told us to be careful and walk in a straight line behind the conductor, not to deviate, because of an electric current in one of the lines. Everybody followed the conductor to the station and got there safely. But it made Mother and me late to meet Annette at the Kings Cross steam engine station, so we had to wait five hours for the next train.

On 17 April 1948, 24 people died when a postal express rear-ended the 17:40 Glasgow to London Euston train. The collision occurred at about 40 to 45 miles per hour. The impact was such that only five of the ten passenger coaches could be pulled away on their wheels. Only the rear eight of the 13 postal coaches could be pulled back. The train stopped suddenly at Winsford when a cord signal was pulled by a passenger; a soldier was seen leaving the train after it stopped. The signalman at Winsford mistakenly reported the passenger train clear of the section and accepted the postal train.. — railwaysarchive.co.uk

Annette's mother was a writer for a magazine and she thought we were on the train that wrecked. My mother didn't know the train had crashed. She had taken the time to do her shopping and hadn't gone straight home. As soon as she heard, she about had a fit.

We, now passengers on the second train, didn't know there had been a wreck ahead of us, but what should have been about a nine-hour trip took 11 hours. With the fire in the tunnel and then the crash, we sat up for 24 straight hours, two young girls, no way to lay back and sleep. We were exhausted. By the time we arrived in Glasgow, we looked like two zombies. I remember Annette saying she'd never been awake so long in her life.

We didn't know about the crash until we got in to Scotland. By that time, our friends and family were worried sick, because very few of the bodies had been identified. My Great Uncle George, the station master at Glasgow Central, found out the earlier train had crashed and by then we were at his home and sound asleep. He telegraphed our families.

Although we weren't evacuated on the early ships to Canada, the bombing became so intense in London and Hornchurch that the authorities finally insisted we children must be evacuated from the entire area. We were sent to many different places north and west of London. Even though we were from near London, and it was a very bad place to be, they evacuated us children to Birmingham—where all the engines and planes were made. One would expect that to be a far more dangerous place. However, it really wasn't. They had few bombings there, fortunately, and I don't know why. I can't answer that satisfactorily. I have no idea how it was decided where we would go.

When Mother found where we were going, she said, "Why in hell would they send them there?" She often used colorful language. She was a plain-spoken woman and if she didn't like something, you would know it. She was never mean, rude, or vulgar, but plain-spoken.

Parents could go with their children in the evacuation and try to find a job there, but my mother was obligated to stay in

Hornchurch. My father ran up big bills and my mother was paying them off. My oldest sister was allowed to stay due to her age. She did not want to go and didn't. I wasn't old enough to say no and neither was Davina.

I remember the day we were evacuated. We had to gather at the school and were taken by car to the train station. Buses were minimal in those days. We rode the first train, then a commuter train, to the main station in London, where big steam trains took the children to the North Country. Mother went with us on the first train. It was wintertime and we were wearing heavy coats, with a label tied to the lapel of the coat, that told our name, age, and where we were from. We rode the first train, then the second train. When we piled on the steam train, Mother wasn't allowed to go. She had to return home and to work. She didn't know where we were going. Well, she knew it was Birmingham, but not where in Birmingham or to whom.

Before the train pulled out of the station, she said something to me that has stuck in my mind all these years. I know she didn't mean it the way it sounded. I was seven and my youngest sister was barely two, a baby. She had had rickets when she was born and a lot of other health problems. Mother was scared to death for us. The last thing she said to me on the train was, "Take care of your sister. If anything happens to her, I'll never forgive you." I have had those words in my head all my life. I'll never forget them. I realized my responsibility at an early age and it weighed heavily on me during those years.

There were hundreds of us on the train. The government was responsible for making sure that schools were empty and that, if the child was going to a family, they still had to make sure you went. I don't know how many schools were represented on our train. I know our town had a secondary school, so there were children on there of another age. I think we had two grade schools in Hornchurch at that time. I don't know if there were any others than that. As the train started pulling out, my mother was weeping and I was weeping because if anything happened to Davina, I couldn't go home. I was petrified. We started off and Davina stuck to me like glue.

What did I see from the evacuee train? The countryside was beautiful, so green even in the winter. There were some little towns and villages. Looking out, I wondered if I would ever see London or Mother again. She was in the bombing area. I had seen the destruction, not just noise, but legs sticking out of debris. Oh, it was awful. And I was more scared by my own thoughts.

It seemed like an eternity. Finally somebody came around with sandwiches and asked if we were hungry. There was milk; I think it was hot chocolate and sandwiches. They said, "This will be all we're able to give you until we get to Birmingham, because there is no dining car on this train. But there's a little fruit, so let us know if you get hungry." Thankfully, Mother had fed us a good breakfast before we left.

We were on the train for six or seven hours. Surely it was not that long, but to a child, hours don't mean anything. We arrived at the train station and they led us off onto the platform. They told us to stay together with our own school and they would take us someplace where we could get a hot meal. That sounded good to me. Everybody stayed together and they came and took us on a bus, like a coach. Buses then were double-deckers, coaches didn't have a second floor. It was dark green, not painted like a school bus, so it was not easily seen from the air. That was good. The Germans could see a nice yellow bus.

They took us to a big church hall, telling us to stay together, trying to get people from each area to stay together. They said, "Stay here and we'll be right back in just a minute and bring you something." They had these tables set up and we sat at the tables. And a few minutes after, the people brought us a nice warm meal.

I was helping my sister. People were walking around us saying, "I'll take that one," just like at a cattle auction; that's how it felt to me. I heard a voice behind me say, "I'll take that one," and I turned around. There was a man and woman pointing at my sister. I said, "That's my sister, we have to go together." The woman said she didn't want two. He said, "We have room for two." But she said, "I don't want two!" They went off to talk and were gone 25 or 30 minutes and we continued eating.

The man came back and said, "We'll take you both." I said, "I thought your wife didn't want us." He said she changed her mind. There was a woman standing by the doorway writing everything down in a big ledger. She took the information from our coats and where we were going. Then the man said, "We're going to my car now." We went with him. His wife was sitting in the car and didn't look very happy. But I still didn't know how unhappy she was. We got into the car and introduced ourselves. He said, "I see who you are from the names on your lapels. Hornchurch, where is that?" He didn't know Hornchurch. I was surprised.

He was a minister of the Episcopal church. Birmingham is an enormous area, probably had 20 churches, so I thought everything would be alright since we belonged to the same church.

It seemed like a 20-minute drive and the wife didn't say much. Their house was on a corner, a beautiful, dark-colored brick two story. It was well kept, a fairly large house. There was a lot of shrubbery. It was fenced, with a big walk and an open gate. I can't tell you the house number, though. It was not very near to its neighbors. There was one neighbor a bit to the left and behind and another a bit to right and behind.

A young girl met us at the door and said, "Oh you're back."

She gave me the oddest look, like, "What are you doing here?" She said, "You have two kids."

Her mother said, "Yes, it'll be alright." The girl gave me another look. It was obvious she didn't want me there. I felt uncomfortable. She was about my age and they introduced her as Joyce.

The father said, "It's been a long day; we need to get them into a bath and bed."

The wife said, "Follow me," and we went upstairs with her. Joyce stayed downstairs. The woman said, "You are old enough to bathe yourself; can you bathe your sister?" I said "yes" and she went to get towels. She said for us both to get in the tub; it was a big tub. She said, "I'll go back and get my husband to take your suitcase to your room." In a bit she knocked on the door and asked if we had our pajamas on. I said, "No, they're in our suitcase." We came out in our towels and went to our bedroom where two beds were set up. "This is your room, and your suitcase is on the bottom of the bed. Do you want me to help you put it in the big wardrobe?" she asked as she opened the door. There were hangers, it was a big chest with drawers. I started putting our clothes away.

She said that when we got up in the morning, she would have to enroll us in school. "How old is your sister?" she asked. I said she was only two, so she said, "Well, she won't be able to go to school. Maybe I'll enroll her in the church nursery." I said that was all right. She said, "Get into bed. You'll need your sleep." I was exhausted. We slept together because Davina was so scared to be away from home and away from Mummy. And I wasn't much of a big sister.

The next morning I heard "bang bang" on the door, and the woman was starting in, saying, "Breakfast is ready. Wash your face and brush your hair. You can come in your pajamas. You'll have time to change after breakfast." She gave me a big bowl of oatmeal. I don't remember if there was any milk in the porridge.

The daughter was there, I knew she didn't like us. She stared at me all through breakfast. Then the mother said, "You'd better go upstairs and get yourself dressed, and you can help your sister dress. I'll take you to school and then I'll take your sister to the church." I helped Davina get dressed and we went down.

The woman said, "You're about my daughter's age, but I don't know if you will be in her class. I think they are enrolling evacuees in a separate class." It wasn't the beginning of school. I don't remember what the school year was, it's different than here. It was winter, but I can't tell you what month of winter. We got enrolled and for about the first two weeks, I think, the evacuees were separated from the other students. They were trying to get us into school with the other kids, and eventually we were absorbed in other classrooms. I was not in the classroom with Joyce. There were several other evacuees, one of whom I became friends with.

On the first day the mother picked us up; we didn't know how to get home from school. She said, "I won't be doing this every day, you'll be walking, so pay close attention."

When we got home, she said, "Go clean yourself up, wash your hands and face, and supper will be served in about 45 minutes." We went back down and her daughter was still glaring at me, giving me the evil eye. The mother said, "I've already eaten, I'll be in the kitchen." There was a wall and a pass through area for the dishes. The table was set and I sat where I'd sat that morning.

I would have called it a breakfast room, but they called it a dining room. Joyce went up and got her dinner and I got mine. The mother went back to doing her chores in the kitchen. On the table was a tray in the middle with condiments: mustard, pepper, and HP sauce, but I never liked sauce. Lea and Perrin Worcestershire, I don't like those. I used to use salt and that was about it.

Joyce picked up something and poured it all over her food. It was like mashed potatoes and green beans and a piece of pork, I don't eat it now, but that was what was on our plates. She just layered it all in sauce. I didn't know what to think of that. Then she covered it in pepper, just poured it all over her food and then she started screaming. I thought, "Why is she screaming?" She was saying, "You did it, you did it."

The mother came around from the kitchen, and Joyce said, "She just took that stuff and poured it all over my food."

I said, "No, she did it herself."

The mother said, "Why would she do that?"

I replied, "I don't know."

She said, "My daughter would not lie to me. If you think it's funny, you'll eat it."

I said, "I can't eat that. I'll go hungry."

She said, "Then you and your sister will go hungry." I did the best I could but I couldn't eat much. It was disgusting. I went to bed hungry.

Joyce started shortly after that showing that she really hated me. It was nothing she said, but what she did to make my life as difficult as possible. She would scratch herself and I'd get punished. I had to go without food sometimes, but as long as Davina got food, I wasn't worried. I wasn't starving, but I began to fear for Davina. She had already had rickets and she couldn't go without food. And Mother had told me, "If anything happens to her, I'll never forgive you." I feared every time I ran home from school that she wasn't being fed. I didn't know how to get hold of food. Finally, I was forced to steal. I knew it was wrong, but I didn't feel bad. I thought I was saving my sister's life. The mother never let on whether she knew what Joyce was doing or not.

I started stealing food from the kitchen at night. I'd sneak sometimes bread or cheese up to Davina, whatever I could find. If there was roast beef, I'd shred some off and package it up as best I could. I'd be careful not to take too much of any one thing. I'd put it in my pajamas in case I got caught and I'd bring it back for Davina and me.

Sometimes, because of my dyslexia, I'd be kept after school. Joyce would go home before me and have Davina on her own. I was not there to protect her. I'm not sure if either of them took it out on Davina. She was always hungry and my mother had stressed that I was supposed to take care of her. I'd ask her, "Did you eat supper?" and she would say no. I worried about starvation. I don't really know if she was not being fed.

My stealing didn't get noticed for awhile, but things just got worse. On the way to school and back, Joyce would pull my hair and kick me. She was bigger than me. She was a bully, just nasty. She said, "You think you can take it? Then I will start on your sister."

In the cafeteria if anybody had anything left over I'd pick it up and take it home. It was a very serious situation and getting worse and worse.

The taste of certain foods and condiments stayed with me for a long time. To this day, I gag at the thought of mustard.

When I talked to my mother, a rarity because we didn't have a phone at home, I begged to come home. She would say, "No, the education minister insisted that you be evacuated." When I wrote to my mother, Joyce's mother oversaw the letters I wrote.

Joyce had a fixation on me and was beginning to fixate on Davina; I guess she thought we were taking up too much of her mother's time. She called Davina retarded, but never when her parents were around.

When they discovered I was taking food, the minister asked me why. I said "I was hungry." He said, "My wife is a good cook," which she was.

I said, "Your daughter keeps putting stuff on her food and blaming me. Your wife makes me eat oatmeal with mustard and pepper. It's terrible, I can't eat it."

He responded, "She wouldn't do that."

He talked to his wife and she said I was a big liar. She told him, "Jasmine thinks it's funny and that she can get her way but she's not."

I argued, "It's not me, it's your daughter doing this." Davina also told them that Joyce was lying, but they just didn't believe us.

We later discovered that a lot of the evacuees were being abused. I wasn't the only one. The evacuees were an unwanted bunch in the school. We had just been dumped on them. There was no orientation or counseling for us, our teachers, or our host families. We weren't up to the same school standards as the other kids were because we had seen so many horrors. Many of us had missed school because of the bombings. There was a difference in our dialects, making for frequent misunderstandings. We seemed ignorant to them. We went into a world we did not understand and which did not understand us. We were a scurvy bunch. Not that we actually had scurvy, which was when you didn't have the proper vitamins. A lot of seamen suffered from scurvy. But we used the term to apply to people who came from the poorest classes, how they used to talk about farm workers here. It was how the teachers looked on us, like we had blisters on our lips, lice, or skin conditions and had been kind of dumped on them. We had the feeling that we were not particularly welcome, although nobody ever said it. But they looked down their noses at us. We felt unwanted.

We didn't make many friends. With Joyce, I felt like I was being held captive. I needed to get back to that big house as soon as I could to keep an eye on Davina. We were so isolated from everyone else. It was like we had a label: I am an unwanted child.

At that time, I had two big fears: one was of losing Davina and the other of losing my mother.

I was talking to my friend at school. She had tried to run away from the home she was in. They had five or six children. The old man would get drunk, pulled her out of the bed, and beat the devil out of her. He did this with his own children. Then the evacuee came, he stopped beating on his children and started on her. She had all kinds of wounds. He bit her, she had cuts, he burned her with cigarettes, hit her with the buckle end of a belt. She was a mess.

I would say, "You've got to tell someone."

She said, "Who do I tell? Who do I trust?" I didn't know either. She tried to run away, and she did a good job, she got out of Birmingham. She was missing for four days. The police were not even looking for her. But she wasn't sure about how to get to London. When the police picked her up, they wouldn't pay any attention to what she said and they took her back to the same place.

Another friend at school was in the same situation, with a family who was not nice to her. "Should we tell our teacher?" I asked her.

My friend said, "Jasmine, we don't know if we can trust her."

I asked my friend if she had any money. "Can I borrow some?" My mother had sent me some stationery and I wanted to buy a stamp. I was going to tell my mother what was really happening. I didn't know what Joyce might do to my sister when I was not there. She could torture her, put her in the hospital.

So I wrote the letter right then and went to the post office and sent it. My mother was there like a shot on the first train she could catch. It felt like I had just put the letter in the mailbox when Mother came up there, angry and worried. She couldn't have had the letter for three minutes before she came. I think she had already called someone in the government before she got there.

We immediately had a court date and they asked me questions. I tried to answer. All the time, the woman of the house was there crying and angry, calling me a liar, and the daughter screaming, "She tells nothing but lies." The mother said these things were not happening in her house. I couldn't concentrate. I was appalled that she wouldn't tell the truth, that they were doing this to us. We were all under oath. There isn't always justice and I do know what that's like. It was very difficult for a child. The main thing I remember is that they were all so angry.

It was very traumatic. I told the judge I stole because I was afraid my sister was starving. The mother was screaming. She was obviously going to protect her daughter, and that's right, you are going to protect your child, even if your child is wrong. It must have been traumatic for the church's parishioners. The pastor's wife dressed up on Sunday and everybody in the church thought she was a nice woman. And she probably was, but in defense of her daughter, she was a tyrant.

I really don't think the minister knew what was going on. He worked terrible hours, he was rarely at the house. A lot of his parishioners were dying in the war. He had a full-time job tending to their families. They'd get telegrams saying their son or husband was badly wounded, and not even where they were. These people were living on hope and fear. It was a very, very difficult time for everybody. He spent more time with his parishioners than his family.

Over the years, I've thought to myself that his wife never knew if he was going to be home for meals or when he might go to bed at 10 and be up and out of the house by 10:30. She didn't know when she would see him again. And she was stuck with two children she didn't want. I tried to forgive her. She told him she didn't want me, and she shouldn't have had to take me. It wasn't fair to her or me. Grocery shopping for these extra children would have been difficult. Shops were a long way and there were often long queues.

When something happens, I try to put myself in the other person's position and ask, "Did I provoke that? Was it something I did?" It doesn't always work, but generally it does and I find I'm partially at fault too. In this case I feel partially guilty for having been the object of unhappiness in their home.

That day, my mother said, "I want them removed and I want to take them home." But it was much worse by this time in Hornchurch. They had what we called buzz bombs, an unmanned bomb with an engine attached. When the engine cut off, it went straight down. They were directed from France and they were beginning to direct them onto Essex.

The government officials said, "You cannot take these children back." They said they'd find another place for us.

Mother stated, "I can't stay here. My boss is really good about letting me off, but I have to work."

The judge said he would schedule a hearing for the next day. He said, "I know several people who might take them. Let me put the word out."

The whole process of moving residences didn't take very long, but I'm really not sure how quickly we were out of the minister's house. Mother probably stayed at a boardinghouse or something like that during this time; I'm pretty sure she only stayed a couple of days. I remember my mother's high-heeled shoes and her dragging me along behind on the walk to the courtroom. Davina didn't understand any of it. She was hungry and Mother was dragging us to meet deadlines.

She didn't know if she was in the right place, didn't have money for a taxi, was just dragging us as fast as we could walk. I don't think our feet touched the ground. She had a saucy little hat, kind of like a robin's nest on her head. She kept trying to keep it on, but she wouldn't slow down. Davina wanted to be carried and Mother couldn't carry her. I told Davina to shut up.

After we were moved, it was like my mother said, "We will never talk about this again."

We were taken from the minister's home and given to a family by the name of Hinsley. They were a couple in their 40s, with one son, who was 21 and in the Army, and the younger son about my age, probably about 7 or 8 at the time. I think we lived with the minister's family for about a year, six months to a year, before we moved.

We were still in Birmingham, but it was divided like Oklahoma City. I'm not sure if they lived in a suburb or not. Their house was a gray brick, two story, like most homes in England at that time. Davina and I shared a room. It was nicely appointed, with nice furniture, good carpeting, and shiny wood floors. Mrs. Hinsley had a nice big dining room and a big oak table. She was a good cook, actually both the Hinsleys were. Everything smelled and tasted so good. Life settled down for us.

Their younger boy had been a blue baby and he had a serious heart condition. He was really a nice kid. In fact the whole family was so nice. The child's name was Barry. He could only go to school a half day, then, after he came home from school and rested, we could play a little. He was very good at board games. We had a wonderful relationship.

Mrs. Hinsley threw good parties. In those days, people didn't have money for food for parties, but she always managed to make a cake for a party. I remember Davina's birthday. I think it was the first cake I ever saw whole. We never had flour or eggs to make such wondrous, extravagant things.

I know her husband worked for the government ministry or something. I'm not sure if he was a supplier for the government or what. His job required traveling. They had a van with the name on the side. While most people had to ration gasoline, he could go get gas in the car, because he took frequent trips out of town for the British government. We could take the van for picnics and such, not large wonderful trips but short journeys. It was so much fun.

The Hinsleys took us on vacation that year. We went to Wales and it was wonderful. The ocean sides were all mined, land mines, but they were marked for the safety of anyone who wanted to go into the water. It was pretty cold, come to think of it, I don't know why anybody would want to go in. The sun was warm. I got sunburned and my freckles came out. We stayed in a little rented travel trailer, with a rounded archway-like entrance with flowers painted on it, like in a gypsy caravan. The trailer was permanently situated on the land above the beach, about a half mile from the water.

Mrs. Hinsley drove us to Wales and her husband came along to make sure everything was alright. He stayed one night and had to go back to work. She cooked sometimes, not always. We ate a lot of fish and chips. For breakfast we had oatmeal and yummy yeast buns, but I don't know if she made them or bought them. She was a very good cook. I couldn't eat enough to satisfy her. She said I was so skinny and I was. I said, "I didn't get much to eat in the last place." "So I hear," she said, and the food kept coming.

We spent the days at the beach. Sometimes she would pick up some fish on the way home and cook it. We passed a little fish market on the way.

There were two ways to get home: straight from the beach, or we could walk up this very narrow lane. There was a farmer who took his cattle down it. The fields were so beautiful and green once you got away from the sand and the beach. The farmer had a young boy take his herd of cows to the grassy fields, then go down and bring them back to be milked. English roads are not straight at all, they go all over the place and sometimes there are hedges growing alongside, so you were kind of hedged in.

Once we were walking down the road and turned the corner when suddenly this herd of cows came at us in a gallop. Mrs. Hinsley said, "Run, run." There was no place to go, there were hedges on all sides. We had come through a gate but we were past that. There would have been no room for the cows to go around us. We kept running and running and she was dragging Davina and Barry, and I was trying to keep up. She was probably in her 40s, but I thought she was an old lady at the time. Her feet never hit the ground and she never looked back. We were trapped with nowhere to go. We couldn't climb over the fence. With two little kids, we didn't have a chance. We had to make that gate. I remember the thundering sound of the hooves.

We barely got to the gate in time. She slammed the gate and we stopped, panting like mad. We stayed there for a long time making sure no cows where anywhere around. We were almost in big trouble. We would have been trampled. I've never experienced anything like that in my life. I think it is the only time in my life that I have been afraid of animals, really afraid.

Mrs. Hinsley had bought fish earlier in the day, but she was so exhausted, she couldn't cook it. From then on, she would send me out first to see if any cows were coming. She would say, "If you see them coming, run back as fast as you can. But stay and listen. You can hear their feet." You could hear them in the distance mooing, but if I didn't hear them coming, there was a good chance we could get to the second gate. It was quite an experience. That must be what it's like to run in front of the bulls. Once the boy got them going, they wanted to get home, and I guess he was urging them on, unaware that we were in front of them. I doubt he could have stopped them even if he wanted to.

The Hinsleys were such a nice family and we had the best time staying with them. But it had to come to an end eventually.

About six months later, again I don't know the exact time, Mrs. Hinsley wrote to my mother and said, "I know it's hard to raise children in the war years and I know you've lost your husband. We have fallen in love with these children. My son loves living with someone his own age, and the children are enjoying living here. We don't know how long Barry may live. Is there any way you would be up to letting us adopt the children?"

My mother was on the next train. She responded: "I'm sure you have been good to the children, but I'll be darned if anybody is going to adopt my children. I don't care if Hitler himself comes."

PART I: A CHILD IN WAR-TORN ENGLAND

Chapter 6

Well, I had loved the country and missed Mrs. Hinsley. It was much more tranquil than life in Hornchurch. There was no one firing on us, no bombs or machine gunning. The Hinsley house was full of love, which was also good, although I had missed my mother. Mrs. Hinsley was a nurturing, loving lady with us, but we still missed our family. So home we went.

My older sister, Helen, had not been required to evacuate. She was in high school. Each day she would come home, my mother would be home soon after. They'd have dinner, then Mother went back to her second job. Helen had to either go to the library to do research or had brought books home. Most nights she would stay home until Mother came home from work. Then they would spend the rest of the night together by the fireplace, which was the sturdiest place in the house and safest from the shock of the bombings.

During this time, some children had returned home from the evacuation, while others remained evacuees until the end of the war. Parents missed their kids even though some of them had been with family. The school had stayed open. When we returned, it was the same situation: we walked to school through bombings and shootings and all that same stuff. We went through the same hazards as before we left. In fact, there were more hazards, because there were more aerial dogfights between us and the Nazis. We were still trying to keep the Germans from going into London.

Coming home from the evacuation, it seemed like we went back in time. Mother took us back to Hornchurch just in time for the B24s and the B17s, even bigger bombers than the others. This was about the time the V1 flying bomb began to appear. It's like a zeppelin, a long, elongated balloon. Also known as a buzz bomb, it was an early pulsejet-powered predecessor of the cruise missile. We had heard about them on the radio and then I saw one. You would be looking at it, then you'd see it falling and the next thing you'd see was the explosion. The whole thing exploded. It made a lot of noise; because of the speed, it left behind a wake of noise. We could hear them in the distance. We could hear that motor when it cut off. It didn't fall straight down, so you'd listen and think, "This one could be bad." You would think you were doomed if you heard the motor cut off and you weren't in the bomb shelter. Then you'd hear the explosion two houses away, and you would feel the shaking of your house and realize you were safe.

They mostly came at night. If the Home Guard volunteers saw them, usually in a spotlight, they would shoot them down; the exploded pieces which fell did almost as much damage as the bomb. My mother would have us cover up with whatever we

The B-24 Liberator was an American-made plane, used extensively by Britain during World War II. The B24 and the B17 are among the biggest of the bombers used during the war.

could and keep our heads down. We stayed away from windows to be safe from debris. Once the bombing started, you didn't come back out to go to a bomb shelter. You had to ride it out. Mother would say, "We will live together or we will die together."

A German crew rolls out a V1, known by Jasmine and others in Hornchurch as the "flying bomb." Also called a "buzz bomb," the V1 was the predecessor of today's cruise missile.

We had to be careful not to do anything that would attract the enemy. If you did have a radio, it was kept very low. All the curtains in the windows had to be closed off at night. We were never to give the enemy any information, even accidentally. If they were flying in the day, they could see. But at night, there were no lights to help them

The B-17 Flying Fortress was another American bomber used by Britain during World War II. With the B-24, the massive plane lumbered through the air wreaking havoc and destruction wherever its bombs were discharged.

navigate. Drivers had to drive with dim, shielded lights. If they heard anything, they had to immediately stop and turn off their lights. There could be nothing to give the pilots indication of where they were—in London or any area close to England. Everything had to be as secret as possible.

Once Britain started bringing in the American bombers, the skies were filled with these big planes. It was a very hazardous time for everybody. We were seeing some of the soldiers returning, specifically those who had been at Dunkirk. Of course, many had died in that battle. If they could, the survivors joined another battalion to stay in the war. Those who had been more seriously wounded came home and took up the duties of the Home Guard, replacing those who were too old to continue serving. Home needed defending too. Some returned to their jobs as firemen or whatever. Most of the fire department was in the Home Guard, as well as the police department, when the officers were not doing police work.

Everybody had more than one job. They got off work, went home, changed into a uniform, and then did something else. When a home was bombed, if bodies were not recovered alive, the Home Guard had to dig them out and get them to the mortuary. Nobody had one job that I can think of. All our neighbors seemed to be working 24 hours a day. I wonder if anybody got any sleep during that period of time? You might see a man at the fire department one day and the next day on the roof or directing traffic. You wondered if he was a fireman or something else. So many people occupied so few jobs.

We had anti-aircraft guns and these big spotlights set at certain points around the city to protect it as a whole. You wouldn't have one on every street. The guns were very maneuverable, they would turn this way and that way. They could raise or lower the barrel of the gun by turning the handle, kind of like a wringer washing machine. The noise they made was like "ack ack ack." You'd see them turning the handle as fast as possible to move the gun. I've often wondered if they can still use their arms at all, if they are alive today. Of course they missed a lot of planes, but they also got a lot of them. When the Home Guard got the planes in their spotlight, and started firing on it, they were usually successful. They could zero in on the lights. We were very well organized and very accurate in knowing how many bombs were coming and how soon they would be there or if they were just passing overhead on their way to London. I don't know if the mayor or the council was responsible, or the people themselves, but everything was highly organized.

Sometimes individuals also had guns. I don't think the wardens carried guns. They had truncheons [billy clubs] to defend themselves if somebody jumped up on them, two way radios, and flashlights to look behind the bushes to make sure nobody was hiding there, relaying messages. You never knew if someone was an enemy. A drunk waddling out of a bar could be the enemy sending messages.

There are no niceties in war. Anyone who thinks there are, is out of their mind. You don't realize how violent it is. Today when you read about a girl running away from her family to join ISIS, she has seen video games, but she has no clue what she's getting herself into. War is a vile, vile thing. War doesn't make kind, gentle people.

Did I see death during the war? Yes, I've heard screams as I passed the homes that had been bombed. I've seen people lying there, the fire department trying to get them out. Sometimes they were still alive when rescuers did get them out. This was an unpleasant education outside of school. It wasn't anything our parents could help, but we did see what happened. There was no way to shield a child from that, walking to school, when there had been bombings just 20 minutes before. You would hear terrible screams, see bits and pieces of the body on the sidewalk. There was no way to shield us from what was happening.

One of the worst things that happened to me was after I came back from the evacuation. I used to walk home with a girl named Enid. We were walking home, and we got to this one area where the road divided. She went one way and I went the other, but we were still not that far apart. Our houses were about a half block apart on different streets. With the bushes and trees, I couldn't see her house. I got to my house and had barely turned the key in the lock when I heard an explosion, and behind me smoke just started billowing. The house my friend Enid lived in was hit. I did not realize this at the time. She had just put her key in the door when the bomb hit the house. The incendiary bomb would burn through the roof, then keep burning through floor after floor until it hit the bottom floor, usually concrete, then explode. Enid's body was never recovered, though bits of her clothing indicated she had been killed.

Mother came in that night and told me that those behind us had been bombed. I saw Enid's house the next day when I went to school. The top was gone. When most houses were hit by the bombs, you think it's going to go up and come back down, but it actually stays in its original position. Bricks and pieces of wood were laying all over the place. Shrapnel, part of the bomb or explosive device, was all over. The interior curtains were ripped to shreds, laying on the ground, bits here and there and somewhere else.

The force of the explosion destroys so much. There was maybe a four-poster bed, which was now bits of wood, bits of the sheet. Looking at the contents, you don't even know what some of it was. It's like putting soap in water and the water takes over, but a bomb isn't that clean. It's violent, like a tornado. It collapses in.

It depends on the bomb and where it hits. Many of the chimneys were left standing when the rest of the house was gone, maybe just some bricks pulled away. But the chimney remained standing still almost like a skeleton in the middle of the building the skeleton of a house. Very little else was left standing. You see some strange sights. It's never the same from one house to another because the bomb comes at a different angle. Some come straight down or the wind carries them. A bomb can drift an eighth of a mile before it hits. It may hit the front of the house and take the whole front. It's really weird. Even a small breeze can take it off target, like a sky diver. And the wind is different at different levels.

Enid's death was a terrible blow to me. It was not until Mother told me about the bomb hitting her house that I realized she was probably dead. I don't remember if they said anything at school about Enid. We shared some classes, not all. I think I remember being horrified and thinking I wouldn't see her anymore, we wouldn't walk home together anymore. I don't recall any memorial or service. I was shocked by her death, but we had to get on with things. There were still more deaths and bombings, but this one was closest to me.

I thought about it a lot as a child. How accurate can a bomb be? Taking into judgment the speed of the plane, the accuracy of the pilot, how accurate can you be? You can't be 100% accurate. They would bomb a half mile off target, but even the slope of the land will make a difference. If they hit that part of the hill first... well there are so many calculations and nobody is that brilliant. Even now, with computers, there are variances.

We tend to rely on everything except God. Man will never be 100% accurate unless God wants him to be. And I think He's probably fed up with all of us. I would be.

Walking past houses that had been bombed and seeing legs or arms sticking up was like having cold water thrown in your face at first. But then it feels like it isn't real; you go into a kind of a coma. It's like when a nurse comes in and she and the doctor give it their all but the patient still dies; well, the first time is disastrous. You feel you didn't do enough. But when you see it day and night, a leg in one place, a body in another, it's part of your own life and you become adjusted. It's a terrible thing to say, that you can adjust to horrors, but it is reality in the worst way.

It's a little like Halloween. They have built Halloween up so it will scare the "h" out of everybody. They've made fantasy look like reality. But reality is forever. We saw much the same things in those awful fields. When you see it, it's sickening. We didn't grow up with the violent television and video games. To us, violence was just part of real life.

PART I: A CHILD IN WAR-TORN ENGLAND

Chapter 7

Several times our house was damaged, but there was never a direct hit by a bomb. One evening we came home and the roof of our home had collapsed. I think it was caused by shrapnel. We knew there had been bombing nearby. Several times we had ended up in neighbors' bomb shelters, or went to things at school and ended up in their shelter, or in the church. You could hear the bombing but had no idea where it was taking place.

This time we came home and tried to open the door; there were no street lights, it was pitch dark. Mother pushed on the door and said, "For heaven's sake, something is behind the door. The hall stand has probably fallen. Everybody get inside so we can turn the light on."

We all were standing there and we turned the light on and saw the damage. There was so much rubble. The furniture, the piano moved a bit. The first floor had cracks on the ceiling. It was better upstairs. When we got to Mother's room, most of the ceiling was still there. But my most prized possession had been destroyed.

My mother had bought me a beautiful doll, with a china head and a body that was stuffed. It had leather arms and its feet were of china. It was expensive. In those days, poor people didn't have dolls like this. Mother bought it for one of my birthdays. It was something I prized. My younger sister wasn't quite as careful with the doll as I was. I would be angry with her and then my mother would be angry with me. I would do my hugging and kissing when I thought it was safe and then put it back up in the cupboard in the bedroom.

My doll had been destroyed in the bombing. I was so mad. I said if I had a knife I would have killed the first Nazi I saw. My mother said, "You might talk big, but I don't think you'd do it." I held what was left of the doll's body and cried.

That night Mom threw one of the mattresses down the staircase, probably mine as it was one of the smaller ones, and we slept on that and on the sofa downstairs with blankets and pillows. We slept from sheer exhaustion. Seeing things like that can really boggle the mind. We knew we were allowed to live another day. I don't know how Mother made breakfast the next day, but we had breakfast and went off to school.

My school was closest to the house, and I was always the first one home. My job was to go in and start the fire, but there were bricks down in the fireplace. "You peel potatoes so I can fix supper when I get home," Mother had said. The kitchen was relatively intact; I don't remember any dishes broken. I lit the fire and it just went boom and all the bricks started falling. It pushed the fire onto the furry rug in front and the rug started to catch fire. I was hysterical. Mother hadn't gotten home yet and I had just put Davina down to sleep. I ran next door to our neighbor's as fast as I could and she came back with me. She brought a huge pot of potatoes and she threw them over the coals. She didn't have time to grab anything else. She managed to wrap the carpet around the fire and it went out.

Mother came in and we started supper. And then we started to clean up the debris. Within three days, things had been replastered and everything was back to normal.

Everybody was really good to keep things in good repair. People would do anything they could to help their neighbors. Our neighbor was an older man, I think he had been an ambulance driver at one time. He was very good about helping out. The windows were almost all gone and he helped us get the glass back in. The back door was all right. The front door had lost the window, and some of the windows upstairs were gone. But within a week we were back in business.

The entire town was in poor circumstances because of the bombing. Those were lean times and nobody had money. We were really poor, but we didn't know we were poor. Once I used the word to my mother and she got angry: "Where did you hear that?" I replied that I had heard some of the kids talking, and she said, "Well, we're not poor."

I said, "Well, we don't have a car." She said, "Does anyone else have a car? Are they all poor?" Cars were not that popular at that time. I never asked or used the word "poor" again. She said, "We always have food on the table. It's a struggle for me to put it there, and I can't always buy the things you want for Christmas or your birthday, but we are not poor."

For five years I wanted a bicycle, and she kept making excuses. She wouldn't say she couldn't afford it. She said I'd eventually get it and it would be a nice surprise.

Mother had to change buses twice to get to work, and the first bus was always on time, but the second one was not. The driver was good about picking up people even if it was not a bus stop, but my mother was frequently late coming home from work. She'd get home and she'd be angry, saying the bus driver was 10 minutes late and she almost had to walk.

Lilian Burchell was everything to her young daughters, Helen, back right, Jasmine, front left, and Davina, front right. After separating from her husband, Lilian worked several jobs to pay off his debts while raising her children, but never admitted to being "poor."

That's what happened to my bicycle. It became the family bike. Everybody used it for errands. I only got it on Sunday and never got to ride it to school. I'd say, "But it's my bike" and they'd say, "You'll get it back."

When I was 9 or 10 years old, my best friend was a boy, Tony Hall. Mrs. Hall's husband was stationed in Africa, Libya I think. There were more boys on our street around my age. All the girls were older or much too young. I remember the first time I tasted peanut butter was at Tony's birthday party. I thought I'd died and gone to heaven.

Frank, who was Tony's second-oldest brother, was always a terrible sleepyhead. His mother could never get him up to get to the shelter in the garden. One time they heard the bomb hit their roof, and he jumped out of bed. It burned through the roof, dropped into Frank's bed, and burned through. When the fire department got there, and they were fast, they managed to put it out. But it had burned through to the first floor. When it hit the bottom concrete floor it would have exploded but the bomb squad got it first. It had burned through Frank's bed. From then on, he was one of the first to get up.

Several times, the Germans tried to sabotage our airport. It was a small airport, but it was keeping their planes from reaching London. They never put us out of action, though. Most of the saboteurs were well trained and spoke good English. They were brought in by plane at night and would parachute out. Sometimes they jumped out too high. They didn't carry oxygen masks, so if they jumped too high, they suffocated before they hit the ground. There were seven or eight of them found, in civilian clothing, but obviously not English. The authorities found various documents on them, showing they were Germans. Sometimes, we wouldn't even have known about it, except they found the bodies the next day.

At other times, they also tried to blow up our trains, which often carried troops back and forth. They dropped bombs on the trains from the air.

We lived in a cul-de-sac so we could ride our bikes without worrying about cars. Tony and I heard that there had been an incident at the station. One train was partially in the Elm Park station and there was a commuter train on the way in. These were electrical trains at that time commuting to and from London. Apparently they were both full of people and a bomb had hit near the station. They were begging people to come help evacuate the wounded. I don't think anyone died.

We decided to go see for ourselves, and we got recruited to help. We got as far as a little Red Cross station or something like that. We couldn't see the train station, but we could see injured people everywhere. A guard with a white band on his sleeve and a red cross stopped us and asked where we were going. We said we were going to see what happened. He said, "Well, aren't you nosey? I'm putting you to work. You're going to take somebody back to the hospital. You're going to let people ride on the back and you'll pedal them." He told us to come back after that, but we didn't. That was scary enough for us!

I transported an injured woman on my bike and I peddled like mad. She had something wrapped around her head, and was bleeding badly on the back of my bike. She was moaning every inch of the way. She held on to my waist with one hand to keep from falling off. I remember being petrified. I don't know how I managed to get her to where she could be helped, but I did. It was about a mile and a half to the emergency aid facility. It was a very good object lesson. I learned at an early age to stay out of the way at an accident scene and not hamper those in need of help.

When we got home, my mother wanted to know where I had been. I was afraid to tell her. Mother was a tiger if you got her angry.

When we were younger you'd better run like the devil if you were in trouble; she would have spanked you if she could catch you. She didn't have a temper as such, but when it came to protecting her children, she did. But she didn't defend you when you were wrong. I got my behind slapped a number of times when I was wrong. She would say, "Don't lie. If you lie to me this time, I will not trust you the next."

If we insisted, "Mother, we didn't do it," she'd go talk to the neighbors or teachers who had accused us of misbehavior.

But she was tough and she wouldn't let us get away with saying it was just a joke. "There's no such thing as a funny lie," she would say. "Go to your room and prepare. I'm going to come in and give you a good licking." You didn't lie to my mother.

So after the train incident, when she asked where I had been, I knew not to lie. Boy, she was really mad because we had to go on two major roads to get there. But this time, I didn't get a licking. When I told Tony that I didn't get a spanking, he said, "I did."

Mother just told me, "If you can't help, stay away." It taught me a lesson and was very traumatic. That was one of my most unfortunate experiences. I will go to my grave remembering riding that bicycle, peddling that woman.

PART I: A CHILD IN WAR-TORN ENGLAND

Chapter 8

With the war and all the violence I saw, it wasn't surprising that scary things were often on my mind. I always thought saboteurs were going to come into my house. Why my house? I had a little bell I put by the door when I was home alone so I'd hear if they came.

People ask me why all the children of that time didn't grow up to be crazy. But we had our parents, who were deep supporters of Winston Churchill and his ability to lead. That's lacking today: the spirit of being able to follow the leader without fear.

People got used to the planes and the bombs. They mostly came at night so we just went on the way we always had. The war showed us the backbone we had always had, but hadn't discovered before. You discover a lot about yourself under fire. That's why there were so many heroic actions. You realize that if you don't help, nobody will, and then you can't live with yourself.

During the war, we got closer to our neighbors, because we shared so much. We realized how much we relied on each other. Like with the wardens, 80- and 90-year-old men climbing on rooftops to keep watch for enemy planes and keep us all safe. We were fighting for our very lives and it was important not to succumb to fear.

Historians throughout the years since the war have debated the "blitz spirit" and Britain's resolute response to the war. They saw that ordinary people found the psychological and physical resources to cope with the bombing. British society seemed to become strengthened by the Blitz and, determined to stay the course. The effect on Hitler was apparently disillusioning. Bombing did not force surrender so he eventually turned his attention to the invasion of the Soviet Union. - theguardian.com

As a result of the Blitz, Britain's health improved, enlistment rates rose, volunteering skyrocketed and patriotism saw a rise, even though more women and children were killed during the Blitz than soldiers until halfway through the war. - prezi.com

Huge social changes took place in Britain in 1940. Along with the strengthening of society's collective backbone, everyone pitched in. "Land Girls," who had hitherto never thought of milking a cow or feeding a chicken, volunteered to work on farms. Women took men's places in the many workplaces formerly closed to them. "Bevin Boys" as young as fifteen worked the pits bringing up the all-important coal to fuel British industry. Whereas Hitler never once visited an air base or bomb-site throughout the war, Winston Churchill, King George VI and Queen Elizabeth (later the Queen Mother) did so regularly, usually being cheered even by people who had been bombed out of their homes. Whatever the outcome of the war, Britain was never going to be the same again. - telegraph.co.uk

During the war, if you went to church, people were assigned a time to attend services. They wouldn't want more than 100 or 200 at most at the church, in case it was bombed. A lot of people couldn't go early on Sunday mornings. For example, the Home Guard, who worked quite late at night to catch the enemy planes going over and bombing the towns, couldn't go early. It was my experience that not many people attended church. Because of Mother's schedule, we went very rarely. We still believed in God and we prayed to God.

Church was important, but most couldn't take time out to go to church. Mother said it was only a building. "God is everywhere" was the attitude we had. The way she brought us up was, if God is in your heart, then God is everywhere.

PART I: A CHILD IN WAR-TORN ENGLAND

Chapter 9

Those were terrible years for a lot of people, not just me. All those people whose husbands never came back or came back so shot up they had to be hospitalized permanently, it was all dreadful. What's sad is that this is still going on in the world now today, too. It's terrible. People don't realize we are such violent people.

Dunkirk was probably the worst part. Everybody was wringing their hands. "My son's at Dunkirk" or "I've got five sons and my husband is dead." Everything was talked about in front of the children. We were not spared the reality and I think we needed to know. Winston Churchill was on the radio all the time. I knew that meant we were in deep trouble. We were not just fighting in Belgium or France. Germans were on their way to England. We would be fighting in our own country. And we were on our own. America didn't come in to the war for two years.

I saw people coming back all shot up. I still wonder today why we haven't outlawed war. It couldn't be just one country, of course, it would have to be universal. But it has to be understood that war achieves nothing, no good comes of war. Alright, we had to go to war. We were already surrounded. But I have studied war. I have listened

On May 10, 1940, the Germans attacked the Allied defenders Belgium, Holland and Luxembourg. Their superior airpower, unified command and mobile armored forces quickly gave the German Wehrmacht the upper hand. By May 12, the Germans entered France, crossing what the French believed to be their impregnable border. The Dutch surrendered and Belgium followed suit.

The Germans advanced in an arc toward the English Channel, cutting off communication between the Allies' northern and southern forces. Trapped by the sea at Dunkirk, the Allied armies in the north were encircled. The Allies attempted a counterattack on May 21, but by May 24., the Germans were ready to take Dunkirk, the last port available for the withdrawal of the British from Europe.

Nazi leaders then halted the German advance. Hitler had been assured by Hermann Goering, head of the Luftwaffe, that his aircraft could destroy the Allied forces trapped on the beaches at Dunkirk, so the forces besieging Dunkirk pulled back.

The lull in the attack gave the British time to organize an evacuation many consider a "miracle" today. Not enough ships were available to transport the huge number of soldiers stranded near the beaches, so British leaders called on all British citizens in possession of any sea-worthy vessels to lend their ships to the effort.

Hundreds of fishing boats, pleasure yachts, lifeboats, ferries and other civilian ships of every size and type braved mines, bombs, torpedoes and the ruthless airborne attack of the Luftwaffe to rescue the men. The Royal Air Force (RAF) resisted the Luftwaffe while, the German fighters bombarded the beach, destroyed vessels and pursued ships. For nine days, the evacuation continued.

By June 4, when the Germans closed in and the operation came to an end, more than 338,000 soldiers were saved, and able to continue the Allied resistance against Nazi Germany. - history.com

As the British were evacuated, they left behind 2,300 artillery pieces, 500 anti-tank guns, 600 tanks and 64,000 other vehicles – about half of the British Army's inventory of heavy weaponry. The loss should have made Britain vulnerable to Hitler's planned invasion, Operation Sea Lion, scheduled for mid-September. Although many believed the Germans did not invade because of the success of Britain's air force, some historians believe Germany's nighttime invasion fleet of destroyers, barges and fishing boats could easily have made the invasion successful.

The British Navy wouldn't have been that effective against an invasion because they had only 14 capital ships in home waters.

Many historians believe that Germany could have invaded Britain by the end of 1940 with little difficulty. But when the heads of the German armed forces could not agree on how best to accomplish the invasion, Hitler decided to turn his attention to invading Russia, throwing away hope of bringing Britain to heel and probably of winning the war. - nationalinterest.org.

to what people had to say and I learned a lot. I know you have to fight back, but not necessarily on the same level. At some point everyone must take a stand, right or wrong. There are more ways to fight back, but unfortunately, these days, everything means war.

My mother drilled it into my head: we were on our own in the war. We are a small little country and on our own. We rode it out for two years. England seemed big to a child living there, but we were and are still a small country. We knew the battle would be our own, so we had to trust each other and help each other. Everyone had to become friends. That's how Churchill kept us going no matter the situation. If you see someone who needs help, go to them and offer. It's a message that has stayed with me all these years—truth, loyalty, dependability. We were all brought up with the same values, the same realizations.

We were actually almost a country of women. From 1939 to 1941, women were building war ships, and we had to be tough and strong. But we also had to be the nurturer of the family. When our soldier did come home, it had to be, "Darling, I'm so glad to see you" and we had to go back to being all sweet and feminine.

Over the years I've taken a lesson from almost everything that happened. It is almost like a parable, people will become either better or more evil during a crisis. I think goodness comes through more often. I've seen people lying dead, but I have never seen anybody going through their pockets. Even as valuable as the identity cards or rations were, I never saw anybody misusing them. I think crime must have gone down during this time. Nobody's home was broken into, nobody jumped in front of you in line. You wish it could be like that again. I don't believe in the devil as such. I do believe in angels. I think the devil is what you allow him to be; evilness is of your own making.

The bombing was horrendous. I don't know how we survived, but we made it through. The U.S. entered the war when the Japanese bombed Pearl Harbor on December 7, 1941, and formally declared war on Germany and Italy on December 11. British and American troops successfully landed on the Normandy beaches of France on June 6, 1944. It was a crucial battle. U.S. troops entered Germany on September 11, 1942.

Hitler committed suicide on April 30, 1945, and Germany surrendered on May 7, my 11th birthday. What a present! We were in London on a shopping jaunt. I don't remember Helen or Davina being there. Everybody around us was jumping up and down and running and screaming, "The war has ended!" Tears were running down my cheeks and my mother was crying too. I told my mother that the end of the war was the best present I ever had.

Churchill declared "Victory in Europe Day" on May 8, ending the war in Europe. World War II was not officially ended until Japan formally surrendered on September 2, 1945. I cried again.

It was an exciting period, England was just coming out of the war. Everybody was anxious to turn over a new leaf and make a new life. We were a country regaining our lives, pulling ourselves together. It was like somebody opened a window and then you could smell the fresh air you've always been dreaming of. Even walking in parks had been dangerous, but now we were free to roam. But eventually we lost touch with everybody we knew in Hornchurch.

PART II: PERFORMER

Chapter 10

During the time when the war was ending, Mother was realizing she had to do something with us children to give us an opportunity for some sort of a career. She didn't know I was dyslexic; she knew I was not quick at math. Boy, was I not quick at math! How I passed was a total miracle. She realized I would need something more in my life. I also had trouble reading until I taught myself to read an entire sentence quickly leaving out small words like "to," "for," "at" etc., then closing my eyes and choosing what small words were needed to make the sentence complete or understandable.

In school I had lots to say and I always looked like I was talking, even when I wasn't. That got me in a lot of trouble. In English schools, they punished you by making you learn lines of Shakespeare or maybe poetry. One time I had to memorize a hundred lines of Shakespeare. Teachers always chose the hardest ones to remember. I had to memorize Julius Caesar about 20 times; I got to know Julius Caesar pretty well. Macbeth, now that's a hard one: "Out, damned spot, out." Who would have thought the old man had so much blood in him? The whole story had so much killing and murder. I learned much of Macbeth too.

My oldest sister had won a scholarship to high school. She was brilliant. Secondary school was for children who were not too bright. I was in secondary school. We had to take an examination to go to high school. If you failed, you would go on to secondary school. I took the test and, of course, I failed. There were two reasons, one was the dyslexia. But also, at this time, I had a large abscess under my chin. My face was so swollen and sensitive, the doctor sent me to the hospital at Romford, the hospital where I had been born. We didn't know what was the matter. I ended up with an enormous lump. It got worse and worse. They decided it was an infection in my recently filled lower jaw tooth; there was a sensitivity in the filling. So I went to the hospital once a week for two or three months while they drained it and tried to heal it. They removed the tooth and the abscess and drained it, but it wasted four or five months of my life going to the hospital by bus. Once I knew the route, I went by myself. But I hated to go, I knew it would be painful. This was in 1945 or 1946.

Because I failed the test for high school, I thought I'd have to go to work in a factory. There is this factory that makes excellent toffee, Trabors. Most of the girls who didn't win scholarships ended up working in the factory, and I thought I would probably have to as well. And it's what my mom thought. But she knew I could sing. There were really good radio programs and my mother had a wicked sense of humor and a lot of nerve. She was calling all these people on "The Morning Show," asking for an audition.

I grew up listening to my mother sing around the house. She had a lovely voice. She was a soprano and could have been a singer. But, because she ran away at 17, she didn't have a lot of time for development of her voice. She adored Jeanette MacDonald and Nelson Eddy movies. We went to the movies when we could. Mother would see movies like the *Sheik of Araby* and be singing those songs all over the house later.

I think I got my voice from Mother. I'm actually a contralto, and sing some soprano, but not high. At one time I could sing soprano, alto, contralto, and bass, a full octave [singing in a deep, rich voice]: "Old man river." But my voice has changed many times over the years, as has my body.

There had been no movies during the worst of the bombing, that would have been too dangerous. But before and after, my mother would find a way of going to the movies on her way home from work. They showed movies in the school, shows like Mickey Rooney and *Our Gang*. They also would show war movies, but generally not to the kids. On a Saturday night, maybe Sunday too, you could go to the school and watch movies there. They tried to keep the numbers down in case of a bombing. Just like for church, they could have five or six hundred people there, but they limited admission at the movies to 100 tickets or so. They wanted to keep it low, so they had maybe three showings a day. Our movie theater in Hornchurch survived the bombing. You would have thought it would be wiped out, because it was pretty tall, but it made it through.

Before my father left, he had bought this beautiful mahogany concert piano. I'm sure it was worth a fortune. It had been used for auditions by the BBC [British Broadcasting Corporation]. Goodness knows how he got hold of it. He didn't have the money, but he bought it anyway. My mother said, "What are you going to do with that?"

He said, "The kids will want to learn to play." She said it was too big for the house; we had to take the dining room table apart to put it in there. All that remained besides the piano was the sofa, two small arm chairs, and a china hutch. My father played the piano a little. Mother said he was full of grandiose ideas.

Helen and I learned to play. When my teacher found I was

memorizing the notes instead of reading them, she would rap me over the knuckles; it hurt. She had no idea that I couldn't see or read the notes. We had a battle going on. If I missed a note—I should have counted them out before I went to the classes—and she realized I was only memorizing, out would come the ruler. I finally stopped taking piano because I didn't like being treated that way. But, I had a good memory and awareness of the notes.

During the times we were home, we always had the radio, and it was always going on about war. We usually gathered in the kitchen where the radio was. When we didn't want to hear any more, or during lights out, Helen would go into the main room and start on the piano. It was a game we played during the blackout. She couldn't find middle C in the dark. Say it was a Christmas song (singing): "No-el, No-el." But once you started playing you were not allowed to change the key, so we sang these awful "Noels." My mother would say, "What in heaven's name is that awful sound?" That's what we did for fun. "For heavens sake, shut up in there," she'd say.

There was a radio show we often listened to called "Tommy Handley and the It Show." I also admired Gracie Fields, who was a singer, comedian, and vaudevillian. I saw her at the train station once when I was probably six or seven. She was so pretty. We all loved her. She had a wonderful sense of humor. "Join in and sing with me," she'd say. She sang a lot of these "keep your chin up" type songs. She'd perform in these bombed areas and where bombs were still falling, then cheer up the troops or just ordinary people looking at the remains of their homes, then go on to some of the training camps and cheer them up as they left for war.

Dinah Shore also sang to the soldiers in America. She did a lot of entertaining of the troops, both going and returning home. Their songs were on the radio. Tessie O'Shea, Kate Smith singing "God

Bless America." Wow, the voice that came out of Kate Smith. She was a large lady, and that voice was so beautiful. Tessie O'Shea was larger than Kate Smith and had a very strong Yorkshire accent. She would say, "I'm going to sing you my favorite song today. Too bad if it's not yours, I'm going to sing it anyway." I loved to listen to the two of them.

A lot of people sang. The news from the front was bad, we were losing so many troops, ships were sunk while bringing back supplies. When we heard the news, everybody sat quietly. Nobody spoke until the news was completely over. Winston Churchill would come on and say, "We're going to be on the run for the first two or three years, but don't lose your spirit, we will be getting them on the run, we will push them with all our might." People walking down the street would still be singing, humming, or whistling. This was the way we kept our sense of humor.

In school we had these uplifting war-inspired songs.

There'll be love and laughter
And peace ever after,
Tomorrow when the world is free.
The shepherd will tend his sheep
The valley will bloom again,
And Johnny will sleep
In his own little room again.
There will be bluebirds over
The white cliffs of Dover
Tomorrow just you wait and see.

We had sing-alongs as well. It's what the troops sang to their girlfriends as they marched away or maybe the girlfriends and wives sang to them.

Wish me luck as you wave me goodbye

Cheerio, here I go, on my way

Wish me luck as you wave me goodbye

Not a tear, but a cheer, make it gay

Give me a smile I can keep all the while

In my heart while I'm away

Till we meet once again, you and I.

There were many of these uplifting songs by very well-known singers in England. There was one, Vera Lynn, a London Cockney, who had some musical training; she was such a cheerful soul. This was a time of camaraderie and boosting morale. No matter how bad it was, they'd always be there to help someone else. It was a tough time. The feeling was mutual—we'll pull ourselves together and that's how we're going to get through this.

At school, my teacher learned that I had a voice for singing. She would tell me to sing when the bombs were falling. I guess she thought my loud voice could cover the sound of the bombs. She probably thought, "Let's find her something she can do." She helped me decide my career.

I had been doing Scottish dances from the time that I was quite young—two or three. My mother thought she was going to make something out of me with the Scottish dancing. But she hated to see me come home from school. My dresses were torn and my hair was a mess. I'd see a boy tear the wings off a butterfly and I wouldn't have it. Even then I hated cruelty. I guess I changed from a tomboy when I was about 11 and I started ballet. When I went to school I had to wear a uniform and they made it clear we had to behave while wearing it.

I had been evacuated at seven and was away for two or three years. Mother would never discuss these things with us later. She felt

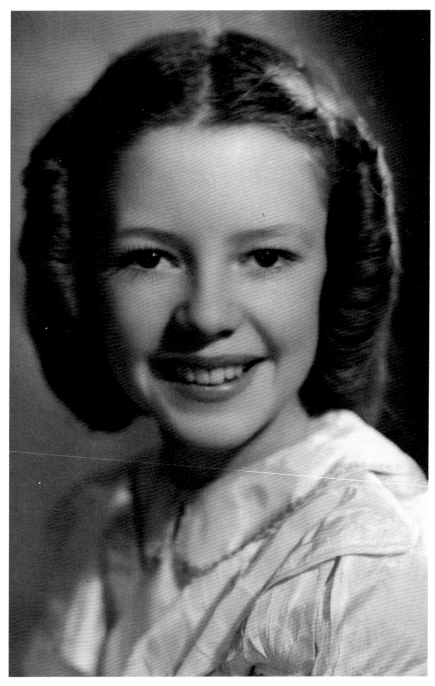

Jasmine at 14 was asked to sing to cover the sound of the falling bombs. Singing, dancing, and telling jokes came easily to her, unlike the difficulties experienced with schoolwork.

guilty for having to let us go, and for the experiences we had. She felt like she should have fought harder to keep us at home. Other kids stayed home and got away with it, I don't know how. The schools never closed down. But she didn't want to discuss it; it hurt her conscience. I didn't feel angry myself, it was just part of life.

My mother decided my life should be in the theater because I sang and danced. She asked for an audition for me with the principal of the Italia Conti theatrical school in London. The school's administration was competitive with the other theater schools. The director had seen me at an audition, but hadn't heard me sing. She asked me to sing for her and said I had a very nice voice. She asked me to dance for her and said I moved very well. She told my mother, "I'll take her on and her fees will come from what she earns." The rest would go into a bank account, which was required by law. She said, "My fees are a flat rate. She may not make that the first year, and may have to make it up the second, depending on what jobs are available." She sent me to auditions quite frequently and it helped my confidence.

Maybe you have seen the *Andy Griffith Show* where they play music on bandstands in the park Sunday after church? They did this in England too, but it wasn't just music. Maybe it would be an act of Shakespeare's *Midsummer Night's Dream* or someone would give a lecture on the history of England. The performer had to go through the Art Board to perform. People would bring chairs and listen. The Italia Conti school would do a show called, *Where the Rainbow Ends* about fairies, happiness, and kindness from doing good deeds. I played in that for a couple of years. The dialogue was very limited. It was mostly movement. They projected a rainbow which comes down to reach the stage. The children gather around and wish everybody happiness and good luck. It lasted about an hour. It was all free, but good experience to expose us to the public's cheering and applauding.

Italia Conti was my whole life then. I made friends quickly, good friends. I was called "Freckles" a lot during that time, because I had a lot of freckles. There were a lot of people at the Italia Conti school who went on to bigger and better things in show business—Anthony Newly, Jean Simmons, Brian Forbes and his wife, Nanette Newman.

I was there from about age 12. The French teacher had a Belgian accent. She spoke French and German. We had five minutes between the French and German classes. We always had to say "Bonjour, Madame." The first morning I walked in, and those who had already been there ahead of me said, "Good morning, Madame Garbelle." I didn't understand, so I said, "Good morning, Madame Garbage." She sent me back to my seat, saying, "My name is Madame Garbelle, not Madame Garbage." I was mortified.

I came out of the two classes not speaking any language proficiently. I was in there for close to a year, but I ended up speaking what I thought was good French, but it was actually German mixed with French.

We had school in the morning, regular arithmetic, writing, spelling, and geography. Then we had lunch, and then dance, acting class, and elocution. We took every available class. One day we might take ballet, tomorrow tap, the next acrobatics, then the next day drama.

The first boy I had a crush on was in theatrical school. He was in my class. His name was Peter. He was very nice, always polite. I don't think he ever knew I existed. I don't know if he ever went into show business. I kind of think that if he did it would have been on the executive side. He was more businesslike than theatrical. He was genteel, always opening the door for you, as well as intelligent. He looked like Rock Hudson, he parted his hair similarly. His hair was very natural looking and he was clean-cut, nice looking.

I went on to another school. My first reciprocated boy crush was when I was about 14. He liked me; I didn't care that much about him. He was a nice young man. But that was it.

My first kiss? In show business you learn to kiss at an early age. We all trained with cameras and microphones and moving gracefully across the floor; it was all part of the training. I don't remember my first real kiss. I think I got to kiss Peter in a school performance.

In acting classes, we had to learn to portray different types of people. We would sometimes have to say such awful things to each other and make it sound as real as possible: "You're such an awful, vulgar man!" "Why would you say such a cruel thing?" or "Don't you know you can't go through life hurting everyone?" We had to practice in front of a mirror and then perform it with the person who would say unkind things back to us. Sometimes you had to cry suddenly; a number of people had trouble with that part. But I would imagine something like the death of an animal or someone I loved, and it almost immediately brought tears. I became an animal supporter at a very early age. All my life it has been important to stand up against cruelty to animals of any kind. I could not stand the thought of any animal being ill-treated.

At that time animals were always missing due to the war. Someone might say, "There was a terrible bombing in my town last night and now I can't find my dog." They might be miles away from the bombing. They didn't find the bodies of people, much less cats and dogs. It would always bother me that the animals were lost or even dead. And no one knew their fate. I have always had pets and I am still very active in animal causes today.

PART II: PERFORMER

Chapter 11

I was about 11 or 12 when I did my first pantomime. A pantomime is a musical comedy, usually a nursery rhyme or fairy story such as *Goldilocks and The Three Bears*, *Aladdin*, or *Cinderella*, made into a stage musical comedy with silly and fun things happening on the stage with musical interludes, sometimes sung or sometimes danced. *The Land of the Christmas Stockings* was one I did in the Duke of York's Theatre. It was about the belief, or disbelief, of Santa Claus during the Christmas period. I played in that show twice with *Cinderella* in between, and *Goldilocks* a year later. In *The Land of the Christmas Stockings*, I wore a beautiful green and yellow velvet dress with white cording.

Most pantomimes were done by child actors. We did *Wee Willie Winkie Runs through Town*, *Peter Piper*, and *Mary Had a Little Lamb*. For "Mary" there was a real lamb, and it

Jasmine performed twice in *The Land of the Christmas Stockings*, in the Duke of York's Theatre, once when she was 11 and once when she was 12. Above, Jasmine is seated at Santa's left knee, with flowers in her hair.

was scared to death. Even in *Goldilocks and The Three Bears*, we had all kinds of characters popping in and out.

One year, as Goldilocks, I must have been about 14, I had several newspaper pieces written about me. One article introduced me as "the youngest leading lady in England" at the time. The lead actress was usually 18 or so. It was unusual for them to use someone as young as me as the lead. They would usually get these young-looking girls to play the role. And usually the male lead is played by a woman in the pantomimes.

Another piece said, "(I)n Feldman's Theatre last night... *Goldilocks and The Three Bears* imbued the mature members with a feeling of good will. Jasmine Lindsay played a winsome Goldilocks.

"Where would pantomime be without the dame, the old granny, always there with a red nose and hair to match? They say every village has one, so this one is where Goldilocks lives. (Granny) twisted the audience around her fingers." Like in the *Beverly Hillbillies*; think of the Granny character. This would be a similar character. This was the whole concept of pantomime: fun and laughter for the children and their families. This was so long ago. Sixty-four years ago.

In the pantomime *Goldilocks*, after eating the porridge in the bears' home, I lay down in Baby Bear's bed clutching a stuffed bear and sang a simple song. It's one I loved then, have always remembered, and sang it to my children and grandchildren, and now even my great-grandchildren. This is how the song went:

Me and My Teddy Bear
Have no worries, have no care.
Me and my teddy bear
Play and play all day.
I love my teddy bear,

He has one eye and has no hair.
Me and my teddy bear,
We play and play all day.
Every night he's with me
When I climb up the stairs
And by my bed he listens
Until I say my prayers.
Me and my teddy bear
Have no worries have no cares.
We play [yawn] and play [yawn]
all day.
Goodnight.

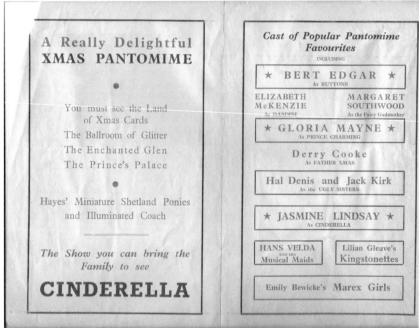

"The fair and charming Jasmine Lindsay" played the lead in *Cinderella* at age 13. Above is a program, front and inside, from her performance in the pantomime.

This is how the local newspaper described me in *Cinderella*: "The fair and charming Jasmine Lindsay made an enchanting Cinderella, with a pleasant face and graceful movements."

However, during one later show, my feet caught in my skirt and I fell right on top of Prince Charming. It was quite embarrassing. Prince Charming was supposed to bend his hand toward me, and I was supposed to take three steps down and take his hand. I was on the top step, came down one step, my shoe caught my dress, I stumbled, and as I fell forward off the stairs I took to the air. They said it was very graceful and looked like I did it on purpose. Fortunately, I didn't weigh a lot at that time, probably 100 pounds. I wish I could have had a photograph of his face as I was coming through the air. The expression on his face was, "Oh my God, she is going to land on me." Neither of us was hurt, but it was shocking.

The cast of the pantomime *Cinderella* jokes around with leading lady, Jasmine Lindsay, 13, far right. A pantomime is a musical comedy, usually a nursery rhyme or fairy story, made into a stage musical comedy.

Jean Marsh, who played the housekeeper in the television series, *Upstairs Downstairs*, played in *The Land of the Christmas Stockings* with me and the little boy who played Wee Willie Winkie went on to fame as a Shakespearean actor. Both went to school with me and both went on to larger fame.

I was 13 when I played in the stage version of *Peter Pan*. It is an odd story; you should read it. I played Liza, who was actually the maid in the Darling household, and she had lost her son. He disappeared and ended up being one of the Lost Boys in Neverland. Liza had a witchy look about her, but more comedic looking. When she decided to search Neverland, she got on a broomstick and literally flew there, wearing a witch's costume. My costume consisted of a dark dress with ankle high boots and under my costume was a contraption called a harness which attached me to wires from my shoulder blades and allowed me to fly.

I was about 5 feet tall, if even that. When I met my son in Neverland, he was a tall boy, and he was reaching and grabbing me around the head and I was grabbing him around the knees with the joy of finding

Jasmine played Eliza in *Peter Pan* at Scala Theater. With wires attached to a shoulder harness, she flew through the audience on her way to Neverland.

each other, bringing a comedic moment into the show. The Lost Boys started finding their parents through Peter coming back and forth. It's a cuckoo story. The man who played my son, Michael Medwin, his name in the play was "Slightly Soiled." He was five years older than me and ended up being a very well-known TV producer later on.

Michael Medwin is probably best known for his film roles as Scrooge's nephew Fred in the musical film version of "A Christmas Carol." He was awarded the Officer of the Order of the British Empire (O.B.E), in the 2005 Queens Birthday Honour's List for Services to Drama. - imdb. com

When James Barry wrote *Peter Pan*, he required that it had to be played in Scala, which was an intimate, small, but well-appointed theater. After the war, the theater, due to some very badly needed repairs not being done, closed for awhile.

Later I started to do some research on Scala. There are all kinds of published books on theaters, but nothing about Scala. I know I didn't dream it. I flew into the audience when I played Liza on a wire and harness attached to my body. Flying was an exciting experience. I've not gone bonkers recalling something that never happened.

One of my friends, a former vaudevillian, and I searched and searched for the old Scala. We were beginning to think we had been living on the Moon, but we knew we

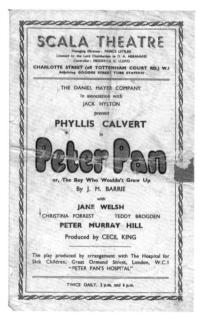

Jasmine kept the program for "Peter Pan," above, for 70 years. She was in the show when she was 13 years old.

were not nuts. I said, "James Barry wrote that story, and when it was made into a play, he wouldn't let it be in any other theater. It was in his will." The theater had some fire damage, so it had to be in another theater one year, and the Barry family wasn't very happy about it. I wasn't in it that year, I think the fire was about two years after I had been in the show.

Everybody kept asking me, "Where was it?" People said it was in Italy, but I said no, it was in London. It was on a particularly well-known street called Petticoat Lane. The street had all these stalls and barrels where they sold goods, not just petticoats. On Sundays an open market was set up in the streets in and around the theater; they would sell jewelry, perfumes, wristwatches, you name it. It was right in the middle of that area. I knew somewhere there had to be a story about Scala.

My friend finally found a book about the theater and sent it to me. The theater had had about five names; they kept renaming it, that's why we couldn't find it. I've kept the book so I can convince myself I didn't go into some kind of coma and dream I was there. It took me a while to realize this new theater was not really new, but the old one refurbished under a new name. It was exciting to find it five or 10 years afterwards.

PART II: PERFORMER

Chapter 12

After the Italia Conti school, I went to the Aida Foster Theatre School. Mrs. Foster made sure the school was properly run by always visiting the classrooms during the course of the day. She would walk into the classroom to make sure behavior was top notch. She also made sure every moment of your school day was filled with activities, not wasted. She was very nice, but very strict. There was no nonsense. She would be up and down the stairs: "What are you doing in the corridor?" If you pulled someone's hair, even as a, "Hi, I'm right behind you" thing, that's when she would get you. "Do you think that was nice?" We'd say, "No, I'm very sorry." She would say, "Will you ever do that again?" We would say, "Oh no, Madame." She was strict about decorum and behavior. You represented her school at all times. We wore socks then up under our knees. She would walk

Jasmine Lindsay, far left, was recognized as one of "Four Bright Girls of Pantomime" in a 1949 newspaper clipping. Jasmine was 15 years old.

around and say, "Have you looked at your socks?" It certainly made me aware of my surroundings. If she caught you with your socks down around your ankle more than once a day, she would give you 10 lines of Shakespeare.

There were times when you had to break out, though. There was one boy in class, I very much disliked him. He finally left me alone after I threw him over a desk. I had long braids, and he would jerk my head back and dip them in the ink wells in the desk. It completely discolored my hair and it wouldn't wash out for days. He lied about me. I can't remember what it was. The teacher thought I'd done something. I had detention for something like a week. He was a real smart aleck. I finally had enough, and I just went after him. I was so astonished I could pick him up. I never realized my strength until I was using it. He didn't tell, didn't want anyone to know. He was embarrassed and very angry, but he left me alone from then on. And the teacher never discovered that I had thrown him over the desk.

I went home and told my mother, I figured I had to. She said, "Why didn't you tell the teacher?" I said he would lie about me and I wasn't about to put up with that. She said, "Did you hurt him?"

I said, "Just his pride."

My mother said, "You're awful."

I replied, "Maybe so, Mom, but I didn't know what else to do." He deserved it. He never blamed me for anything after that. In fact he stayed away from me. It was the best way to deal with him. He was a bully. I'm sure he bullied other kids, too.

If you humiliate a bully, it stops them. But something has to snap in you to do that. And it did. Then you have no control. I was lucky everyone had cleared out of the room. I think several kids knew. He had gotten away with too much for too long. It's so funny the things that come back to you.

My friend Tony lived three doors down from me. There was a boy who lived across from him who bullied everyone. He always called Davina, my younger sister, names. So one day I pushed him down and he fell on a horseshoe with a rusty nail and let out the awfulest scream. His mother was livid. She had to take him to the emergency room of the hospital to get the horseshoe extracted. Nobody else felt sorry for him. They all went off so happy. "Mother," I explained. "He was giving Davina a hard time." All I did was rush at him and push him. I had tried to ignore him but finally he made Davina cry. I felt this was justified. And again, he didn't bother us any more.

Helen and I went to dance classes taught by a man who had danced with my mother years before. One of the male dancers fell sick and the instructor asked me to dance the reel and represent Scotland in England's International Dance Festival. It was a man's part and I said, "No, I won't do the man's part, I don't know it."

Jasmine is pictured here, far left, during a dance practice at the Aida Foster Theatre School. In front of her is her friend, Patsy Ann Hedges.

He said, "I'll teach it to you. You'll be so petrified, you won't forget anything." And he was right. He showed me two or three times, but we only had a few minutes to work. Then he pushed me on stage. I was so scared. The dance requires that you hit the back of the leg in the calf area twice

Lilian Burchell's daughters were all taught Scottish dancing at a young age. Helen, far left, Jasmine, second from left and Davina, far right, dance with a girl whose name they have long since forgotten.

with the opposite foot. He told them all to keep pushing me to where I needed to be each stanza.

It all worked out well. I was so fortunate to dance in the festival. I saw many dancers from many countries. I was so enthralled by the skills of dancers from Poland, Russia, and some Scandinavian countries. This added to my enjoyment and my later interest in country dancing, which represents the international dances of each country. I received a letter several weeks later saying I was in a photograph in *The New York Times*. I never got a copy, but my friend said she recognized me because of my long hair. I was surprised that a picture of myself made it to New York because I was not a true representative of this particular Scottish reel.

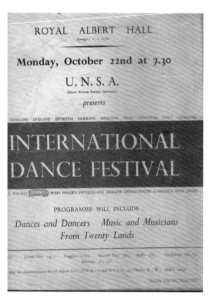

ROYAL ALBERT HALL

Manager: C. S. Taylor

Monday, October 22nd at 7.30

U. N. S. A.

United Nations Student Association

presents

DENMARK ENGLAND ESTHONIA GERMANY HOLLAND INDIA INDONESIA ITALY LITHUANIA

INTERNATIONAL
DANCE FESTIVAL

POLAND SCOTLAND SPAIN SWEDEN SWITZERLAND UKRAINE UNITED STATES of AMERICA WEST INDIES

PROGRAMME WILL INCLUDE

Dances and Dancers   Music and Musicians
From Twenty Lands

Jasmine was invited to participate in the International Dance Festival in about 1947 when someone else was unable to attend. The festival programme is among Jasmine's historic collection.

Italia Conti and Aida Foster kept me working. They wanted their fees and I was on contract. But I didn't stay to graduate from Aida Foster because I started entertaining at aerodromes and military hospitals with my sister Helen.

There was an agency who took people to entertain the troops with Scottish singing and dancing. Performing at hospitals and the aerodrome was something Mother had done when we were growing up. Even though her hours at work were dreadful, sometimes she would slip away on her way home to sing a couple of Scottish songs to the new recruits. Maybe she'd stay a half hour and come home.

Helen and I got an invitation to entertain at Queen Victoria Hospital. Scottish dancing was very popular at that time. We went on for five or six months to various places doing Scottish singing and dancing. We would sing some comedic or nostalgic songs, like "After a couple of drinks Glasgow belongs to me" (singing a funny old Scottish song by Will Phyph). Our audience would laugh at the lyrics about someone who drank too much and sometimes they joined in the singing. We didn't get paid, but it didn't matter, it was our donation to the war effort. Sometimes the audience would give us something, a souvenir or a button, but there was never any money exchanged. I think we were the first entertainers who came to some of the places we went. This was just barely, barely, barely after the war.

The first time we went to Queen Victoria Hospital, we hesitated when we went in. We knew it was a burn hospital, but didn't know much else about it when we arrived. There was a marble floor and patients were wheeled in. Almost all we could see were eyes looking out of bandages.

I wasn't sure that I could do it. The patients could barely move, but they reached out their hands to let us know they'd enjoyed our performances and they said thank you for coming. They enjoyed it so much. It was hard to dance and sing seeing these legs and faces all red and burned... and their tears...

Jasmine, in full Scottish dress, entertained soldiers at Queen Victoria Hospital as an early teen. "My mother thought she would make something of my Scottish dancing," she recalled.

Anyway, the officials asked us to walk around and talk to the patients, and my sister started and I followed in, walking about. I still remember one man who was so nice. He said he had a Scottish background and hadn't heard Scottish singing in years. I asked, "How long are you going to be here?" and he said, "I don't know. I've been here six months now, I don't know how much longer. I'm not that old, just 22." It broke my heart.

In one case there was a man lying in bed, and all you could

see were his eyes and you couldn't see anything under the sheet. Sure enough, he didn't have any legs. He had crashed landed in a plane and they had pulled out what was left of him. He had one arm, a trunk, and what was left of his face. I thought to myself, what kind of life will he have with no legs and one arm? And, obviously, his face was all burned, as it was all swathed in bandages. It was so tragic to see these people. Sometimes you see people who are cheerful and they seem to have no reason to be. These young men were thanking us, but we should have been thanking them for serving and saving us. You never know what the future will hold but they all seemed eager to continue their lives despite their pain. They had serious injuries, but still made plans for their futures. When I came out of the hospital, I felt like I had been hypnotized.

It was a really rude awakening and it nearly killed me. That was probably the most devastating thing in my life. It made me grow up a lot. I later came to see that I was fortunate to have this experience, but I was about 13 at the time and it was very traumatic. I am still amazed by it today. From this I learned that where there is life, there is hope.

I guess I had lived in a rose-colored paradise. I knew what was happening. I saw the explosions, saw the planes hit. But, you know, the reality...I took it to bed with me. It bothered me for a long time.

Right now in Bosnia, kids are watching their parents being shot or stoned to death, and they must relive that moment again and again. It will be with them the rest of their lives. It's awful.

I can't understand why people keep going to war. When you see the devastation to people and to their land...how can they go back and do it again? I don't want the TV on. I don't want to see any more, I have no desire to know. I've been through all this, and watching again is sickening. Why don't we learn anything from what we've been through? And nowadays, everything is entertainment. They have to go over and over and over it until we're mired in it. I don't know what has become of us. It's on every program. Violence isn't entertaining to me. I am appalled by it.

So I saw what happened to people when they come back from war, all shot up. In the beginning they didn't have many special hospitals for very badly burned people. Archibald McIndoe started a burn unit at Queen Victoria Hospital for pilots coming back and people who were in tanks when they burned up. He wasn't a knight at the time, but the queen knighted him for his work with severely burned people. These people thought they'd never join society again. It started as a hospital to learn and discover and investigate how to treat burn victims.

Archibald McIndoe was born May 4, 1900 in Dunedin, New Zealand and in 1930 moved to London to become a clinical assistant at St. Bartholomew's Hospital. In 1938 he was appointed consultant in plastic surgery to the Royal Air Force.

When World War II broke, McIndoe moved to the recently rebuilt Queen Victoria Hospital in East Grinstead, Sussex, and founded a Centre for Plastic and Jaw Surgery. There, he treated very deep burns and serious facial disfigurement like loss of eyelids. He not only developed new techniques for treating badly burned faces and hands but also recognized the importance of the rehabilitation of the casualties and particularly of social reintegration back into normal life. He disposed of the "convalescent uniforms" and let the patients use their service uniforms instead.

Important work included the discovery that immersion in saline promoted healing as well as improving survival rates for victims with extensive burns—this was a serendipitous discovery drawn from observation of differential healing rates in pilots who had come down on land and in the sea.

After the war, McIndoe received a knighthood in 1947 for his remarkable work on restoring the minds and bodies of the burnt young pilots of World War II through his innovative reconstructive surgery techniques. - historylearningsite.co.uk

During one of the last visits, Sr. Archibald came out to thank us himself. He said something like, "It stirs my blood to see this Scottish dancing and how it gives pleasure to these patients." I wish I had gotten to know him. I was so impressed by him and the work he did.

We talked to a lot of the men who had been through the horrors of war. Most were so brave and wonderful. I've seen people with many more problems than I have. Those were very sad years, but good for me. They made me very strong. And they made me very thankful that I am who I am.

I remember crying on the bus on the way home, thinking about those poor men and their crooked burned smiles.

PART II: PERFORMER

Chapter 13

I drew my strength from looking back on my past. I think that's why I became the family crutch, meaning they could lean on me. Everyone did, even my oldest sister. She was so careless, always late out of bed. She often left for school half-dressed. We traveled to school on the train. We were living in Priors Park then; it was a two-story home. She would run downstairs and grab a piece of toast. I'd say, "Hey, that was mine," and "You'd better hurry, we have to leave for the train. I'm leaving without you." She usually got her clothing on, but was always in a hurry to get the rest of herself together. She'd get the buttons done on the way. We never missed the train, but we'd have to start running.

Helen would ask if I had brought my practice shorts with me and she would say, "Give them to me, I need them." I would have to practice without my shorts. You usually wore a pair over your underwear in the color of your dance costume. She'd say, "You've knickers on, and your costume comes down over it."

I'd say, "When I twirl, my underwear shows." I got in trouble several times during practice because I didn't have the dance shorts.

"You'd better have the dance knickers on tomorrow or I'll fine you," Miss Shandley, the ballet teacher, would say. She carried a golf club and would tap your legs lightly when you were working at the bar if your back or legs or arms weren't in position. She never fined me, but would make me stay late and work at the bar.

In 1948, Jasmine also modeled clothing for a Kidditogs Ltd. catalog. She was about 13.

I'm the reliable one, the one everybody turned to when they had a problem. If my younger sister had problems with kids at school, I'd tell them, "I'll punch you." I became used to everyone depending on me. It started when I was seven and I had to take care of my sister during the evacuation, and that never altered. They would probably all agree if you asked them. I don't know if they were even aware of it. Helen would say, "I hope you have money because I don't have anything for the fare, I spent it yesterday." So I had to bail her out, and most times I didn't get it back.

I got used to my role as the family crutch and felt good about it. Our Scottish name meant "very trustworthy." It probably comes from there. My mother was the trustworthy one in her family. She didn't have brothers and sisters, but other relatives and friends knew they could come to her if they had a problem and she would do whatever she could. I've seen her lend money when she couldn't afford to. I guess I took her role. I didn't realize until this book that I became the family crutch.

Yes, my mother was colorful. She could say things in Gaelic, I don't even know what she said. If we were having a fuss, I'd just let it pass. Mother could always make you feel you were needed. She needed you to be good because she was having to worry so much about finances and the war. We needed to do the things she asked of us. I know I wasn't easy to raise; I questioned a lot of things. My mother went through a lot she shouldn't have had to go through.

We knew very little about our father's family, the Burchells. We never really knew our father. I've researched his name. My mother wouldn't talk about him and I didn't blame her, he was a rascal. What she actually said was, "May he burn in hell." So I wasn't going to ask any more questions. But once she was dead, there was a wonderful place in London, Somerset House, a kind of place of records, it's called St. Catherine's now, but we visited it to try and sort out my past.

Once when my husband and I were flying home from Germany, the pilot came on the loud speaker and said, "This is your captain, Captain Richard Burchell." Now this isn't a common name, even in England. There are names like Smith and Jones, but not Burchell. I asked Melvin, "Did I hear right?"

He said, "I think he said Burchell."

We had a male attendant, and when he came back, I asked

if there was any way I could find out if the captain spelled his name with an "i" or a "u." He said he was busy serving the meal, but before we landed he would try to find out. And I wanted to find out whether he came from where my family lived, this one area that I'd already discovered. I said, "If he comes from Watford, I'd like to meet him if possible."

Sure enough, 15 minutes before landing, the attendant came back and said Burchell was spelled with a "u" and he came from Watford. "If you sit on the plane after it lands, he will visit with you," he said.

I said, "Wouldn't it be funny...."

And Melvin said, "Jasmine, don't get your hopes up, your father has been all over the country," which was true.

When the plane landed and everybody got out, we went up to the cockpit and I took one look at him and burst into tears. I said, "I'm so sorry, but you look so much like I remember my father. He died when I was five, and I've never seen a picture of him, but he was about your height, about six foot six, dark hair, blue eyes like you, and I hate to say it because it's rude, but he had a nose like yours."

He said, "Well, my mother and father never got married and my mother wouldn't talk about him. I only know he was a rascal and he used to go back and forth on the train from London to Scotland."

I said, "Could you be my half brother? Could that be?" I'm sure he was. I said, "I am not trying to get anything from you, I doubt very much that there is any family inheritance. My last memory of him was when we entered the hospital. He had piercing blue eyes like yours. You look so much like him."

He said, "My mother wouldn't like to hear that." The pilot was making a return trip to Germany. I said, "I know you don't have time, and I'm being met and they'll wonder what happened to me, but I'd like to talk to you some more." He said to contact him through British Airways. I said, "Are you sure, you won't give me your address?" He said, "Well, I'm not from here and I'm back and forth, but they can always get hold of me."

He would have been about the right age, about four years younger than me. I think he was already in his 40s. He thought I was a loony, I'm sure. It took awhile to dry my eyes. The copilot was wondering if I'd been drinking. It's one of those stories you read about but don't think it could happen to you.

I went back and did my research and there were little Burchells associated with my father all over the place, quite a number of them. He was one of those people who couldn't keep his hands off women. He was good looking, I guess that's what made him the beast he was. He was several years older than my mother. He did marry her and didn't marry the others, so that's something.

I tried to contact the pilot, but he never wrote back. My letter may have gotten lost. I tried again and put my return address. I said, "I'm not interested in your financial dealings, I just want to know if you know any more about your past. I would like to fill in more about my past and thought maybe you would want to fill in your past with me. I would be happy to fill in anything I could." But the letter never came back. Captain Burchell obviously did not want to fill in the past.

Jasmine Burchell would have been a better show business name than Jasmine Lindsay, if people could spell it. I even had people spell it "Birdchill." I finally gave up trying to use it. My mother had a very good friend with whom she went to school and did Scottish dancing, and his wife was a dancer. She had just died, and we went by to see him. He was such a lovely person. My mother said, "My daughter is in show business and is doing quite well."

He asked, "Do you use your Scottish surname?" I said I used

Jasmine and sister Helen became close when they both were performing as actors and dancers. They toured together in *Me and My Girl*.

my father's name, which was Burchell. He said he had never known my father's name; he too knew he was a rascal. He asked, "How do you spell it?"

I said, "This is why I'm going to change it."

He said, "If you do, remember I have a lovely name and no children." His name was Lindsay, and sometimes they spelled it "linseed." I didn't think anyone in England could spell. But I thought it was such a pretty name, so I took it. I never met the man again, but I hope I honored his name.

We were distantly related to a very famous Scottish entertainer, Harry Lauder. Helen changed her name to Lauder. So we both had Scottish names. We were proud of our ancestry; they were ordinary people, no flair, but good people. They were happy and that's one of the most important things.

PART II: PERFORMER

Chapter 14

There have been times in my life when I didn't know which direction I was going. If you really looked at me I was the most impossible person to be in show business. When I was a child, I was skinny, scrawny, freckle-faced, with straight hair and knobby knees. If you passed me on the street, you'd never notice me. But I was so "go get 'em," that's what pushed me off. My mother helped me. There are stage mothers who take their kids to all the auditions and make sure everybody sees them; usually they are too pushy. I went to the auditions by myself, starting when I was about 11.

In auditions, sometimes the casting director would talk to me about what I was supposed to do, but in general, we were on our own. They might ask, "How old are you?" or "How do you spell the last name, do you go to one of the theatrical schools?"

I'd say, "Yes, I go to Aida Foster."

They'd ask, "Do you have someone accompanying you? What are you going to do for us today?" If you were good, they'd say, "Please stay, I'd like to talk to you" or "Thank you very much, we may be able to use you in another show." You can't be right for every part.

As I got older, I learned more and more about auditions until

I developed a routine. First thing you do is put on a facade. You're not the girl who got out of bed this morning, combed her hair, and went on to audition. You're not that girl any more. You are a dancer or a singer or whatever the producer wants you to be. You're putting on an act. And then when you arrive at the audition, there are usually a lot of people there, some really tall and glamorous young women. You look in the mirror and say, "I don't have a chance. If they're looking for glamour girls, I'm at the end of the line. If they are looking for talent, I may have a chance."

When I went to auditions, I generally sang musical comedy-type numbers, something like, "I hope I'm going to have a date tonight." At least they remembered me when I left. It's so much easier to have a comedic act. The second time I came, I might sing the serious song. This was my defense, I guess you might call it. I just enjoy leaving the audience with a sense of fun and enjoyment. People remember you when you're funny. So many people are up tight, so nervous at auditions. It's the worst thing you can do. They are looking for someone to engage the audience, and audiences can be tough.

Competition is enormous. And many young women are insecure. When rejected for a part, sometimes they will cry as they leave the theater. I often would intercept them to tell them not to feel rejected because they didn't get a role. "You must not have been right for this show. Try again for another show. It doesn't mean you're not talented. You're just not the type of talent they need for this show. There are other auditions."

Some would say, "I've been to five auditions this week, and nobody asked me back."

"Well, maybe it's just that the leading man isn't tall, and maybe they don't want tall girls around him to make him look short." I never went home feeling depressed. They just didn't think I was what they wanted, maybe next time. Don't give up too easily. You can't take rejection personally.

People in show business act like they think they look okay, but inside they have so many insecurities. We look at ourselves in mirrors and think, "Oh Gawd, is that me? What happened to my hair?" We are very self-effacing; we don't have all the glamour most people think we do. When I went to auditions, I'd see girls with legs to the Moon and I'm short. Sometimes they sent the girl with the long legs home. I'd see large-busted girls and I'd think, "If they're looking for large-busted girls, I have no business here." Then sometimes they'd be weeded out, too. When you've seen all the girls you thought would get the part sent home, you think, "Maybe they needed someone short, not necessarily so much on top. Maybe they need someone with a good singing voice. Maybe they're looking for me after all."

I always had a strong desire to succeed and have always been hopeful to the end. I inherited hope. I don't think I'd be where I am today if not for hope. My mother always thought there would be a better tomorrow and that's the way she brought us up.

The first audition is the worst. You look at all these people and think, "What the devil am I doing here?" I have seen people walk out of the door without waiting for an audition. You shouldn't do that; you don't know what they are looking for. It might be you, but you've already made the decision yourself. You see really gorgeous girls come in and disappear out the door. You would think they would have found a part for her no matter what. Obviously, gorgeous isn't enough.

I never had curves. I thought of myself as the ugly duckling. No, my mother didn't say that, she thought I was gorgeous, as all mothers do. But "to thine own self be true." I can't disguise how I was, I had freckles, I didn't even know when I arrived at puberty. I thought I was one of those kids who would never amount to anything. I had several friends who were really gorgeous and I hung around them in hopes I would appear attractive too. One was with me in *Me and My Girl*, Greek background, beautiful, everything I wanted to be. Wavy black hair, gorgeous face, lovely smile. Then there was one who played the lead in another of the shows, five foot two, beautiful natural blond, petite little figure, but, oh, what a figure. I thought, "Oh, what I'd do to look like that." I was noticed because I was with her. She attracted every boy in town.

Mother couldn't really tell me I was beautiful because it was a lie. I'm honest with myself. She went to an audition with me once years later, after I was in Oklahoma. It was for a show at the Lyric Theater. She was feeling uncomfortable when she saw other people coming in to audition. She looked around and said, "We'd better go."

I said, "Why?"

She said, "You are much too old. These girls are younger than you." She was embarrassed for me. Thought I'd be a flop or something.

I started laughing and said, "Mother, these shows have cast members of all ages. I might end up being the mother or great-aunt of one of these girls." She didn't know what to expect and she was really worried. She didn't want someone to be rude to me. When I got into the show, I did play someone's housekeeper. The play was *Oliver*. Most everybody knew me. Many years later, the orchestra leader at the Lyric Theater said, "You always surprise me. You always say something silly, something I'd expect from Phyllis Diller. I never know what to expect from you."

I once saw Maggie Smith of *Downton Abbey* being interviewed. The interviewer said something like, "You must have been so beautiful when you were younger." Maggie Smith, with that dignified, aristocratic air she has, glared at her and said, "Get real." I nearly fell out of my chair. That sounds like everyone in show business.

Maggie Smith really wasn't pretty, was she, but she has a very unusual face. You see all her thoughts on her face.

My sister Helen had an agent and she had landed me a role in a traveling show, *Me and My Girl*. She said, "They're looking for chorus girls." But back then you couldn't go on tour at the age of 14. Helen said, "You look older." Which I did. That's when I added a year to my age and I got taken on the show. When the curtain went up, it began with all the musical numbers from the show being played by the orchestra, then the show began with my sister playing the lead. Helen had the first vocal number. She was always late and I often worried that she would not be there when the curtain went up. I would get dressed as fast as I could for my chorus number, have her costume in my arms, hair brush, and anything else she might need so I could get to the wings of the theater and help her get on stage in time for her number. I remember always wondering if she would make it. I wouldn't know where she was. I'd be standing there in makeup and everything else, ready to go, when she'd be running out. She would be pulling on her dress and I'd be brushing her hair. She would be sitting on anything to get on her shoes. It was dreadful but we managed to get her on stage in time.

The Lupino family, who owned the company, was of Italian descent and they had worked for many years in vaudeville. In vaudeville, you sing, dance, do everything. If you're told to do something, you do whatever you're told. They had several generations with experience in show business. The famous movie star Ida Lupino was part of the family. In *Me and My Girl*, the male lead was Lauri Lupino Lane and his aunt played the elderly duchess; she was aristocratic looking and very dignified, similar to Maggie Smith. She had traveled all her life and been in very good shows. She was like Ethel Barrymore, she had that dignity. She never went without gloves.

Jasmine, right, and a friend on the promenade of a seaside resort in England while traveling with *Me and My Girl*. The show toured all over England and Wales.

When she was onstage, you looked at her no matter who else was there. Well, the aunt decided she did not like my sister, who was not disciplined enough to be on time. After three or four months of barely making the show, she fired my sister.

I thought I'd be fired, too. She called me into her room and I thought, "Here it comes." She said, "Your sister is fired but you're not.

If you want to remain, you can tell your mother I'll keep an eye on you, make sure you are safe." She didn't know I had lied about my age. I was only 14, but she thought I was 15.

"You are very young to be traveling on your own," she said. "So you can assure your mother that I won't let you get into any trouble. I'll make sure you don't," she added with emphasis. And she did. She would ask, "Aren't you supposed to be in your dressing room?" "Aren't you supposed to be on stage?" There was certainly never any hanky panky or flirtiness on my part or anyone else's. She made sure of that.

I was the one who told my mother that Helen was fired. She said she was not surprised. I also said to Mother, "They said I could stay, that they will keep an eye on me." Mother said, "I trust you. The money is good. Stay if you want." I was surprised Mother didn't make me come home.

It was a pity Helen lost that job. Helen was very talented and beautiful. She had a petite little figure, everything to make it in show business, and she had a brain, but not for business. She sometimes missed cues because she wasn't there. She never missed her lines when she was on stage. That woman gave her several lectures: "Either shape up or your understudy is going on." And that's what happened. Her understudy got the job. And so I traveled extensively through England for the next several months.

Show business is a world of make believe and, hopefully, when you visit it, you become your character, but remember it is not real. When you leave, you leave it all behind and return to your own persona, which was difficult for some people to do.

Helen returned home and did some repertory theater, a small company of actors who put on plays for the local residents. Usually they do dramatic or well-known plays. My sister was a very good actress, and worked a lot in television later.

In *Me and My Girl*, we went everywhere, all over England, to Wales, not to Scotland, but Southampton, Kent, all over the country, playing different towns every week. We were a cast of about 20, but it must have seemed larger to the audience, because everybody did quick changes and we all had other duties, selling flowers or serving as doormen.

On Saturday night we would do the show, pack up our costumes, and on Sunday morning we'd meet at the station to catch whatever train. Usually we were not going too far. Sometimes it would be an hour and a half or more, but usually short trips. We had these great big trunks to pack the costumes in, as well as our own suitcases. We were not responsible for the trunks containing the show's wardrobe, but we had to carry our own private suitcases.

We had roll call at the train station. When we'd get into the new town, we had to find our boarding house or hotel where we would be staying the week, then be at the theater about 8:00 a.m. Monday and work with the local orchestra until early afternoon. You'd do all your dancing and everything, go through the whole show, then eat something light like a chef salad or soup and be back at the theater by 4:00 p.m., ready for a performance Monday night.

We were packing a suitcase and moving every week, staying in comfortable, but not attractive, nice places, sometimes cold and damp, or boarding houses. All the places that take in people for a week, one-and-a-half or two pounds was the going rate for a bed and breakfast. We paid out of our own pocket. The company was not responsible.

Usually you started calling to get a room a few days before you arrived. Sometimes a girlfriend would share a double bed. She'd cook one day and I'd cook the next. One time, one of the other shows that had been there the week before was staying over so I couldn't get a room anywhere in town. I kept calling and people kept getting back to me: "Sorry." "Sorry." "Sorry." Someone had said I could sleep in the bathtub, but I wasn't eager about the idea.

When the train arrived in the city where we would be that week, it was pitch dark, raining, and cold. I went straight to the police station. I walked in and told them I was looking for lodging. They said, "Oh boy, you're going to have a heck of a time. You can try, but I don't think there is anything open." There were three or four people on duty. They said everything was booked as there were two plays in town and a circus coming next week.

I said, "I may have to stay the night at the police station. Or I could always go back to the train station and sleep on a bench there." They said, "We have two extra cots back there and you're welcome to one." They sent me back to get my luggage. The police station was as comfortable as any place.

The policemen in charge said, "You can use the toilet here. We'll make sure there are fresh towels." I spent the night there and in the morning a policeman brought in a big tray with hot tea, fried eggs, bacon, potatoes, and toast. For heavens sake, I'd never been treated this way in my life. I'm a dancer so I'm not used to people waiting on me. It was great. It was much more comfortable than I had expected and everyone was so kind to me.

In the morning, they said, "Get dressed and come out when you're ready and we'll try to find a place for you." A policeman came back before I was dressed and said they had found a place. "I don't know how good it's going to be," he said. A police car took me to a boarding house and the room was nice. I got to stay there for the week. The landlady said, "I'm not letting you walk home at night," so her husband picked me up each night after the show. And the week was most pleasant.

I told Mother I'd spent the night in jail and she said was shocked: "What did you do?" and I said I didn't do anything. She said, "Well, they don't put you in jail for nothing."

"Mother, let me explain."

Years later, I told my husband, Melvin, "I've a secret to tell you. I'm a jailbird."

He replied, "As long as you didn't do anything bad it really doesn't matter." I explained the full story.

I remember one Christmastime when our tour group was staying in a lovely home in Cumbria's Lake District in northwest England. The cast always tried to stay together when we could, but it wasn't always possible. This time there were about seven of us. It was a big house, set in the hills and surrounded by fir trees on the edge of Lake Windermere. There were velvet draperies and Tiffany lamps. We were walking home from the show together. It was the last night of the show before we went home for the holidays, about three days before Christmas.

Coming home from the show, it was snowing so beautifully, quite large flakes. It was cold, but not freezing. We were all arm in arm going home, singing in the snow, something about snow for Christmas. There was no other sound, it was so quiet, just our feet crunching in the snow. The next morning we would be on our way home to spend Christmas with our families. The setting was so beautiful; I can see it in my mind now.

We all had our supper and went to bed thinking we'd arise early and get ready to catch our train to go back to London. But in the night it snowed so hard; it turned into quite the blizzard. When we went downstairs in the morning, the landlady said, "You're not going anywhere. Have you looked out the window?" None of us had.

"Even I'm not going anywhere," the landlady said. She had been planning to go south to her daughter's for a month. "We don't have provisions and there is no way of getting out of the house to get more. We will have to call the police."

When we went to the windows in the dining room, we couldn't see anything. They were under snow. We went upstairs and looked out and the snow was up to the second floor windows. There was a big garden and the lake was frozen. There were no trains running, everything was closed down and we were all stranded. This had all happened in about four to six hours.

The boarding house had a two-way radio and the innkeeper called the police and told them all these people from the show were stranded. This is when I found that England had a machine called a helicopter. I had no idea what a helicopter was, but there were one or two at the air base in the Lake District. The landlady called the police and told them the problem and asked if they could get food to her. She was able to keep the coal and wood fires going to keep us warm. They made arrangements with the air base nearby to send a helicopter to deliver food to the lodge.

We woke up the next morning to this awful sound; you could hear it five miles away. Not knowing what it was, we all ran to the windows. The house was vibrating and suddenly this strange looking thing appeared in the sky. It looked like a washing machine with wheels and a whirly thing on top. Or like a large bomb with whirling blades in about three places. We said, "What the devil is that?" It turned out to be our rescue machine. They were talking to the lady on the radio and said they would drop food in the yard. They couldn't get close to the house. We would have to dig our way to the food. Then the door came up and all these arms stuck out, throwing food.

While the women looked out the windows, the men grabbed shovels and tunneled their way towards the food. The women were hanging out of the windows, screaming, "Too far left, go right." Finally we saw heads come up and they got the food and came back inside. They had to make several trips to get the food; it was well boxed up. There were enough supplies for about a day and a half. I can't really remember what the food was. I think there was Spam and corned beef to make sandwiches. We had porridge [oatmeal] for breakfast. We went through the whole ordeal again two days later. The snow had melted some, but not enough to get out.

On Christmas morning we were looking out at the snow and it was beautiful, but we were all wishing we were home with our families. It was the first time I had been away from home for Christmas. Everyone was feeling depressed. From the smells, we knew the innkeeper was doing the best she could to make a nice dinner. She called us downstairs and said, "I know you don't have presents, so we ought to make some." She had all kinds of material, yarn, embroidery thread, all kinds of sequins and little buttons. We sat in front of the fire and she showed us how to make several things. We used yarn to make little men with yarn legs and arms; we put silver elastic around the necks, and a pin so it could be put on a coat. I had made them before. She had us sew on eyes and a mouth. Some of the mouths were lopsided. She gave us really good ideas on what to make each other. We sat there for three hours messing around with the material.

We would close our eyes, put the little gifts behind our backs, and pass them on to the next person. We kept passing them until the person who didn't have one got one.

The husband made us hot chocolate and we played gin rummy. It was really nice. The innkeeper made it so pleasant. Sure, she was depressed too, not being with her family. But what started out looking like a depressing day ended up being fun, with everybody laughing and having a good time. Now I couldn't tell you the innkeeper's name if my life depended on it.

Finally the snow melted enough that we were able to catch trains home. We were about two days late for Christmas Day with our families, but we were glad to be home. I had missed my family, but I learned a lot about being on my own.

PART II: PERFORMER

Chapter 15

I was so mean to my stepfather; he should have slapped me. He was such a nice man and I was such a suspicious kid. I thought he was a Lothario trying to get my mother's money. She had no money. You have no idea what goes through a child's mind. He brought money into our house. My older sister was worse than I. My younger sister, Davina, accepted him readily. He told us he'd never had children and Mom came in with three, two wary,

Michael "Mike" Geselle was a good thing in our family, but he joined it when I was 13, which is not a good age for a girl. Mother had been widowed from the time I was about four and a half. We'd had our mother all to ourselves. He was 11 years younger than she; we thought he was a real gigolo.

My mother met my stepfather through his brother,

Mike Geselle married Jasmine's mother when Jasmine was 13. He was "a good thing in our family," Jasmine recalls, although she also remembers being "suspicious" of him.

Frank, who was passing through the aerodrome at Hornchurch. Frank got out of Poland just in time. He didn't like his job, coal mining, and he got called up by the Polish army, just barely before the Germans came. Frank and the other soldiers came to England and formed their own battalion in the French army. He spoke some English. Their orders were to go to Scotland to train.

At the aerodrome, he had heard Mother sing. I don't think he'd heard Scottish singing before. Frank talked to Mother and wrote to her for awhile. He was happily married and wasn't interested in my mother. Mother loved to write. She would write 20 letters a day if she had time. There wasn't a lot of entertainment, so mail was very important. That was all there was to do, that and listen to the radio, maybe get to the movies once a month. My mother was a good writer. Frank was transferred almost immediately to Scotland.

Mike came from a poor family. He was Polish born and brought to France at the age of three. While he was still a teen, still in school, he had been captured by the Nazis and forced to work in a coal mine. The Nazis wanted to increase production in coal. They took kids from school and made them work in the coal mines in France. Many were killed due to lack of knowledge of safety measures, like not shoring up the ceilings of the mines. Mike managed to escape. He said he was not going to live that way and escaped to England. If he had finished his education, Mike would have been a brilliant man. He joined his brother's unit until the end of the war.

My mother was getting married and my soon-to-be stepfather, although he spoke many languages, couldn't get a job in Hornchurch as a translator. There was nobody to translate for. He drove for the funeral home for awhile, but could make more money as a translator, so they decided to move to London. I went with them to see several houses. They chose one and moved while I was on tour with *Me and*

My Girl. I had to find them when I came home. Every house on that street looked the same. I teased them, saying they were trying to lose me.

My stepfather drove a cab and he would try to pick us up when we got off work. Sometimes he had a fare and couldn't. If he couldn't pick us up, we had a two-mile walk home from the train station. There was one night, about 11:00 p.m. as I was coming home from a show, when I got off the train and, a half mile from the station, I heard somebody behind me. It's not unusual for people to walk in London, but this one seemed to be coming behind me too fast. I didn't like the sound of the feet. They picked up speed, almost to running. It was very dark. The lampposts were quite a distance apart. This was London, where Jack the Ripper had lived. I had just seen that movie so it was fresh on my mind. My imagination went wild. My feet felt like two concrete blocks; I was in high heels and couldn't run very fast. Then there was a hand on my shoulder. I wheeled around and a man said, "Miss, you dropped your glove." He put my glove in my hand and walked on. I stood there for four or five minutes, still trembling. It was kind of nerve wracking, but all he was trying to do was give me my glove back. My knees continued knocking the rest of the way home.

Show business is kind of intense. When you know a show is coming to an end and you have to find another one, your concentration goes back to your agent or whoever is getting you your jobs. It's going to be a whole new world. It's a changing life. When my tour with *Me and My Girl* ended, I started looking for something else. Between jobs I would often work in retail with my mother.

Mother had left the knickknack shop by the time she moved to London. My stepfather was making much better money and my mother was working at Stone's, a very prestigious department store. The owners were a nice family and, when I was between shows, they let me work there, primarily selling in the handbag area where my mother worked. Mr. Stone was very proper. He walked through the store several times a day. He said I had a nice demeanor.

One of the other salesladies named Dorothy worked at the counter across from the handbags, and she and my mother covered for each other when one went to lunch. During Mother's lunch hour, if I ran into trouble while there alone at the counter, I would ask Dorothy. She understood that I was not too bright in math.

One day, a woman came in with this fabric bag and pulled out this purse. It was an absolute mess. She wanted to return it. She said she had only had it 12 years.

Jasmine took up the last name of Lindsay in the 1940s as she continued her career in show business. With wavy red hair and an infectious smile, she used personality and talent to pave her way.

It was a crocodile purse. They probably cost the equivalent of $1,000 now. The purse looked worn out. I knew it was expensive, but why would I give her a new purse for that old thing. I was thinking, "Are you crazy?" I mean, I would have been embarrassed to bring it back. But my mother came up about that time and explained that it had a lifetime guarantee, and 12 years was not a lifetime. Twenty-five years was not a lifetime. They kept the names and addresses of all the buyers of these expensive purses, but Mother had a memory like an elephant. She recognized the purse and helped her get another one. Really, it looked like it had been run over by a Mack truck or in the water by a submarine. I didn't say anything rude, but I would never have given her another purse. I would have suggested she put it in the garbage. I don't think I would have been working there for long if Mother hadn't come up when she did. The lady left the department store happily with a new purse.

I worked for Stone's for a few years on and off when I was between shows, then I got a chance to work at a "cooperative" store, like a general store. It sold everything except food. The money was pretty good and it was much closer to home. They sold nylon hose among other things. During the war, this was the number one item that women wanted. Hosiery was rationed, and it was as valuable to ladies as makeup. Stockings were stronger then and didn't run like they do today. With care, one pair could last from four to six months with only a few snags. They cost probably $5 or $6, which was like a $100 today. I had no idea how dangerous it was to work in the hosiery department.

Before the 1920s, stockings, if worn, were worn for warmth. In the 1920s, as hemlines of dresses rose, women began to wear stockings to cover their exposed legs. Those stockings were sheer, first made of silk or rayon [then known as "artificial silk"] and, after 1940, of nylon.

The introduction of nylon in 1939 by the U.S. chemical company DuPont began a high demand for stockings with up to 4 million pairs being purchased in one day. Nylon stockings were cheap, durable, and sheer compared to their cotton and silk counterparts. When America entered World War II, DuPont ceased production of nylon stockings and retooled their factories to produce parachutes, airplane cords, and rope. This led to a shortage and the creation of a black market for stockings. At the end of the war DuPont announced that the company would return to producing stockings, but could not meet demand. This led to a series of disturbances, with hundreds, sometimes thousands, of women descending on stores trying to buy the stockings. The disturbances became known as the Nylon Riots and continued until DuPont was able to ramp up production. - smithsonianmag.com

When stockings arrived, we would have to secretly unload them. On one occasion, we were not allowed to put them out for sale to the public for two or three more days. When the lady in charge of the counter went to lunch, a woman came in and told me, "I wanted a pair of nylons." I said, "We don't have any."

She argued, "Don't lie to me."

Again I said, "We really don't have any."

She said, "I don't believe you. You are absolutely a liar."

She was a big woman and she grabbed me by the neck of my blouse and pulled my upper body over the counter. "I said I want a pair of nylons and I'm not leaving without them," she said.

I said, "I'm sorry, ma'am." She dropped me and I nearly fell on the floor.

About that time our floor walker came by; she grabbed him and said, "That woman is telling me a barefaced lie."

He looked at me in desperation and said, "Go get her a pair of nylons."

I said, "But, but..."

He said, "Stop arguing with me and go get a pair of nylons."

I'm standing back so she wouldn't grab me again. He said, "Go." I went to the back and brought out a pair. I didn't even look at the size.

"And how much are they?" she asked. I told her. She said, "Get me another pair for my daughter."

I said, "We're only allowed to sell one pair to a customer."

"Are you going to argue with me?" she said. When I gave them to her, she paid and walked out of the store, holding them up and telling everyone, "They have nylons today."

When the other salesgirl came back, we were inundated by 500 customers. She asked me what happened, but I didn't have time to tell her. We sold every pair of nylons in two hours; I don't know how many pairs there were. Everything was gone. We were just exhausted. When I got home, I told my mother, "I am not going back to that shop. They nearly killed me today. People grabbed me and pulled me over the counter."

Mother said, "I don't blame you for not going back." I wouldn't even go back for my paycheck. I had no clue who that woman was or how she knew. Maybe she saw us unloading the nylons.

PART II: PERFORMER

Chapter 16

I was having a wonderful time in show business, not making a lot of money, but enjoying it. Since I had left the theatrical school, I had been on my own and I had very good luck and seemed to find jobs relatively easily. But I decided I needed an agent.

Agents won't take just anyone. You have to show them what kind of a performer you are and they decide whether you will be a good asset to them. Generally, they would know this if you had been working in and around London. If you tell them you've been touring with this show for six months, most would know the shows and the kind of performers in these shows, so you already had a reputation. If you'd been working six months, obviously you did well. They didn't replace you. Agents will still want to know what kind of talent you have: can you really sing or maybe your dancing leaves much to be desired. Their reputation is at stake, too. If they say this girl can do anything and then when she comes out she's a dead loss, it hurts them.

I went to see an agent. It was a partnership and I liked one of them. I started to realize what a jerk the other one was after he asked me back for an appointment late in the evening. It was in an office building. On the first floor everybody had gone home. When I got to his office, he asked me in. I realized what he had in mind when he reached around me and pushed the door closed. He started moving toward me and he followed me around the secretary's desk, which was vacant, of course.

This is what is known as the "casting couch." I have seen the casting couch one or two times, but there was only this one time I was literally running around the desk. I learned what the casting couch was by the time I was 15. I was so stupid; I don't know why in the devil I went to the late appointment.

I said, "I'm only 15 years old and you had better not lay a hand on me." He came to an abrupt stop. I remember him looking shocked. He thought I was older. I said, "My mother will come after you. She won't stand for this kind of behavior. You won't have to worry about the police. My mother will kill you."

He said, "I see," and that stopped him cold. We had no more problems whatsoever. The agency took me on as a client.

The other partner, Bill, who ended up being my agent, was so nice, such a gentleman. I asked, "Why in the devil are you tied up with him?"

He replied, "He's not really that bad."

I said, "Yes he is. I tried to keep him in line, but you really need to put a muzzle on him."

I would never have gotten in trouble because my mother held those ropes tight. I grew up with the thought that you must respect yourself. Mother would say, "You can become a drunk, lying on the curb, people walking past you and kicking you. Then how will you feel?" She would never let up. "I may not be there to see, but somebody will be," she would say. She should have been a preacher. She always came up with the right admonition to get my attention.

People have such a bad opinion of people in show business.

They think all show girls are sexually aware, slept with everyone. But most of us wanted to keep our reputations, marry somebody, have a wholesome marriage. At least that's what it was like in my day. You tried to maintain as much dignity as possible. I can't talk about how it was later.

My agent, he had glamorous pictures taken of me in various scenarios, but never undignified. When a part came up, he could send photographs out and they would call me to go to auditions. The photographer that my agent used was very renowned. He had photographed Queen Elizabeth when she was young. He was very good and very expensive. I paid about a half year's salary for those photos and they were good. I wondered if they were really me. Especially when they had me wrap up in a shawl, I looked glamorous even to myself then.

One time, my sister and I, who were with two different agencies, went to the same audition. We were told to dress as sexy as we possibly could. I had a sweater

Jasmine spent six months' salary on her publicity shots. The photographer had once taken pictures of Queen Elizabeth.

pulled down, a skirt so tight I could hardly move, and really high heels. I looked as cheap as I could. When I walked across the stage for the audition, the man conducting the auditioning said, "What's your name?"

I replied, "Jasmine Lindsay."

He asked, "How old are you?"

"Eighteen," I said.

"Are you going to sing for me today?"

And I said, "If you want me to."

I sang a few bars of some song, and he said, "You're not quite right for what I want; you have a nice voice, but you're just not common enough." I was not sure how to take that.

He said pretty much the same thing to my sister. We thought, "My gosh, how common do you want us?"

It turned out he was casting for the theater show *Sweet Charity*, the Neil Simon play about an ever-hopeful dance hall girl. Honestly, we walked out of the theater and started laughing. We thought we looked so terrible. It's a good thing our mother hadn't seen us. She wouldn't let us leave the house like that. She would have said, "I'm not going to let the neighbors see you."

We walked a half block hoping we wouldn't see anybody we knew. Then there were these two young policemen behind us, and they were whistling at us. I said, "I don't think that's allowed while you're in uniform, is it?" We were not sure if they were trying to pick us up or arrest us.

Helen said, "Just keep looking ahead."

We walked into this restaurant for lunch. We decided to treat ourselves, we hadn't eaten out for awhile and this place made wonderful food. The waiter gave us a look and said, "Are you ladies waiting for someone?" We said we just wanted to be seated. So he seated us, and in a few minutes he came back and said, "My friends and I are going to a waiters' ball tonight, we'd like to take you both." My sister was married at the time and we laughed and laughed. He said, "Have I said something wrong?"

We said, "No, thank you for the invitation but we aren't available."

The producers didn't think we looked cheap enough, but two policemen tried to pick us up and two waiters wanted to take us to a waiters' ball. I don't know what kind of ball it could have been, as cheap as we looked. When we got home, we were still laughing. My mother said, "Where have you two been? You look dreadful." When we told her, she said, "Why didn't you tell me, I would have had Michael [Jasmine's stepfather] drive you." But it was already too late, we laughed and laughed.

My friend was in the British cast of *Oklahoma!* I auditioned for the role of the smallest child, but I was still too short. I tried again about six months later for the taller of the children. By then I was too tall. Ironically, I ended up living in Oklahoma and I've been very

The marquee for *Excitement*, a Latin quarter show in which Jasmine danced, glitters outside the theater. Fantastic costumes and even some nudes highlighted the 1949 show.

happy to be here. When Mother and Michael had a wedding anniversary, I got them tickets for the show. Afterwards Mother said, "What a load of rubbish." I was so hurt. She didn't like all that jumping up and down. For someone to have children in show business, she was very conservative. I guess I should have been used to that.

Another show I worked in was a Latin Quarter show, *Excitement*.

I was one of the dancers. The Latin Quarter shows had nudes. In England, if they had nudes, the FCC laws said you couldn't move, couldn't even blink your eyelashes. You had to stand like a statue. I was a dancer, though; if I went nude they would have demanded their money back.

Our costuming was fantastic: sequined top, split skirt. Then when we turned around, under the ultraviolet light, our back looked like a whole other person. The hat was designed with a face on the back, the split skirt made us look like a girl with short underpants and long legs. We had on fishnet hose. You danced facing the audience one moment, then switched back with these exotic movements. The split skirt was lightweight, but when you turned and flipped around, the sequins would catch the hose of somebody else and rip them. We called that split skirt a tail. "Your tail ripped off half my right stocking," we'd say. We had to go to wardrobe a lot. Three months in the show and they had to replace the stockings frequently. The costumes were beautiful, Lord knows how much

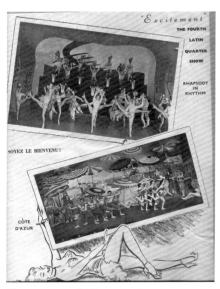

The programme for *Excitement* is among Jasmine's collection. Jasmine is front right in the top photo and far left in the bottom.

In *Grin and Bear It*, Jasmine sings during the "Salome" number. The show was another Latin quarter production during the late '40s.

those costumes cost, and very functional, except that it was weird to dance with half your pants hanging on another girl's leg.

I weighed about 87 pounds at the time; the hat weighed maybe 78 pounds. It was very much like the pineapple Lucille Ball wore on her head in that 1955 episode when she played Carmen Miranda. We were supposed to walk very gracefully coming down the stairs. You could hold your head to the side, but don't trip. If you started going backwards, you kept going that way.

I was about 15 in that show, maybe 16. Boys said we were knockouts. I wonder if we really were. There was only one man in that show, wearing a suit like ours, the back of the costume gave the appearance of being another person. The audience loved it; it was a most unusual production and beautifully choreographed.

Jasmine, center, performs with the chorus line in *Grin and Bear It*, in 1950.

Jasmine in another costume during a performance of *Grin and Bear It*. Although only 15 years old, Jasmine told producers she was older to get the job.

PART II: PERFORMER

Chapter 17

Jasmine's copy of the programme for *South Pacific*, signed by several members of the cast. She joined the cast in the early '50s when she was 17.

Richard Rodgers and Oscar Hammerstein's *South Pacific* opened on London's West End at Theatre Royal Drury Lane on Nov. 1, 1951. The cast, which changed several times over the 802-performance run, included Mary Martin of *Peter Pan* fame, her son Larry Hagman, who later starred in American television's blockbuster series *Dallas*, Sean Connery, Millicent Martin and 17-year-old Jasmine Lindsay. On the day that Jasmine auditioned, there were 300 others vying for parts. Jasmine won one of the two roles chosen that day. She played Ensign Pamela Whitmore, a small speaking part in the chorus.

South Pacific had recently opened in Theatre Royal Drury Lane when two cast members dropped out and replacements were needed for the roles. I auditioned and won one of the two roles, along with one of my of best friends, Carole Leslie. We didn't know each other that day, though. We started the show together and shared a dressing room.

It's a beautiful theater, goes back to 1663, the time of Charles the Second. During the Great Fire of London, it caught fire in the middle of a performance. While remodeling, there was another fire.

I shared a dressing room with Carole, Millicent Martin,

Jasmine, right, during a performance of *South Pacific*. Playing Ensign Pamela Whitmore, she sang that she was "gonna' wash that man right out of my hair."

A Christmas card shows the outside of the Theatre Royal Drury Lane as it appeared during Jasmine's run in *South Pacific* during the early 1950s. The theater was first built in 1663.

The Theatre Royal Drury Lane was founded in 1663 by Thomas Killigrew under a charter granted by King Charles II. The first building held 700 people. The second building, seating 2,500, opened in 1674 and was reputedly designed by Sir Christopher Wren. It was demolished in 1791 and rebuilt with a capacity of 3,611. It was destroyed by fire in 1809. The current building was designed by Benjamin Wyatt and opened in 1812, with a capacity of 3,060, although auditorium changes have reduced this now to 2,184. - Through the Stage Door, Theatre Royal Drury Lane.

and three or four other girls. We had a wonderful cast in *South Pacific*, probably one of the best of any show ever. They were all good, good people and we liked each other. Usually, there will be some jealousy that causes problems, but not in this show. We would probably have died for each other. I don't recall anybody saying anything negative about anybody else, at least not about anybody in the show.

Jasmine met her lifelong friend Millicent Martin, second from left, in *South Pacific*. Above the two are shown in a recent photo with their spouses, Melvin Moran, right, and Marc Alexander, left.

Millicent Mary Lillian Martin was born June 8, 1934 in Romford, Essex [just one month and one day after Jasmine was born in the same hospital — a fact the friends never realized until late in their lives.] Martin is an actress, singer and comedian. She had her own weekly BBC series in the 1960s and received Tony nominations for *Side by Side by Sondheim* (1977) and *King of Hearts* (1978). Television roles include her recurring role as Gertrude Moon on the NBC sitcom *Frasier* (2000-2004). She starred with Julie Andrews in *The Boy Friend* on Broadway in 1954 and with Michael Caine in the 1966 film *Alfie*. - imdb.com

I became very close to Millicent Martin during our time in *South Pacific*, a relationship that has lasted a lifetime, over two continents. We still correspond regularly and we have visited each other in Oklahoma and California frequently. In fact, she came for the 2016 Jasmine Moran Children's Museum banquet and we sang a duet together.

In *South Pacific*, there were five of us in each dressing room, so we had to become close. Dressing rooms were not glamorous places. They were tacky looking, with clothes hanging all over, makeup everywhere. We'd write notes to each other and ourselves on the mirror with lipstick: "Don't forget to help Joan with her bra" because she can't get it done while jumping out of her shoes. The dressing rooms weren't dirty, but untidy, about what you'd expect with five girls doing quick changes. The dressing rooms were fairly good-sized. They had built-in cabinets and chairs pulled up to built-in dressing tables with mirrors and shelves. There was a place at one end of the room to dress. There was a rack of clothing. As you took something off, if you didn't have time to put it back, you'd put it on the back of a chair—never the floor—and do it later before you left for home. There were two dressing rooms next to each other. Most of the costumes were light and airy, although some were heavy. The wardrobe mistress would say, "I spent hours sewing on all those sequins; it had better be on a hanger when you're done." Even in touring shows, costumes were not carelessly flung around. Each rack held a set of costumes for one scene, and there was another rack for the next scene.

You saw bums [backsides] everywhere after awhile. Sometimes you'd have to change on the side of the stage and the wardrobe mistress would come help you get into the costume if it was a really quick change.

In *South Pacific* I had only four lines to sing solo: "I'm gonna' wash that man right out of my hair." It was just one step above the chorus, but I would have done the show for free or even paid them it was such fun.

Muriel Smith, the woman who played our Bloody Mary, was wonderful. Her voice had such timbre in it, such resonance. It stays with you. Timbre makes the voice so beautiful. She sang "Bali Ha'i may call you," so beautifully and she did it in such a way you could hear it calling you. It's not just singing a note, it's singing with feeling. It's not a vibration. A lot of people go like they're being shaken by the throat. She didn't, she really had it. When she was doing her numbers, I usually tried to listen. I always stood in the wings to hear her. I felt inspired and so pleased to be in the same show with someone so talented and so sweet.

She was black, but she played the part of a mulatto, a person of mixed black and white ancestry. Muriel was a combination of French and Irish and the American south, maybe some Creole. She died of cancer in 1985 at the age of 62. One of my friends from England let me know that she died. I wish she had lived much longer. She had so much talent.

Muriel was the best Bloody Mary I've ever seen, and I have seen five or six versions. She had a voice, the laugh was so deep and rich, you joined in laughing too. She had kind of

Muriel Smith was an American singer who portrayed Bloody Mary in the London West End production of *South Pacific*. Jasmine said "our Bloody Mary" was the best she has ever seen in the many reproductions of the show.

a strange life. She was telling us all at a party, "I've never met anyone I wanted to marry. Well, there was a boy I went to school with that

I thought I wanted to marry. I was always half in love with him, but he never looked at me. I found later he'd married someone else. My mother keeps trying to get me married. The first thing she asks men is, 'Are you married?' I would come home from a show and I'm tired and look like the devil and there is my mother saying, 'I've got a surprise for you.'" I don't think Muriel ever did marry. I loved her mother, too. She was such a character, kind of like Whoopi Goldberg in nature. She could have been the mother of any of us.

There's a movie about the 19th century Parisian artist Henri de Toulouse-Lautrec; it was made in New York. Zsa Zsa Gabor played the cancan dancer, the woman he loved. Muriel Smith was hired to sing for Zsa Zsa and she did a beautiful job. I went to see the show and people all around me were saying, "I didn't know Zsa Zsa Gabor had such a gorgeous voice." I turned around and, in a loud voice because I wanted the whole theater to hear, said, "That woman couldn't sing like that. That voice belongs to another woman, and her name is Muriel Smith." Everybody was looking at me. She didn't get any credit for it either. I had to stand up for her. Muriel Smith had a voice in a million. How could they think that was Zsa Zsa Gabor? It was too much for me.

> Muriel Burrell Smith [February 23, 1923 – September 13, 1985] was an American singer. She moved to London in 1949 and performed in productions of two Rodgers and Hammerstein musicals at the Theatre Royal Drury Lane as Bloody Mary in *South Pacific* in 1951, and as Lady Thiang, the King's head wife, in *The King and I*. She was the unaccredited ghost singer for Zsa Zsa Gabor in John Huston's 1952 movie *Moulin Rouge*, a biography of Toulouse-Lautrec. She is perhaps best known in the UK for her 1953 No. 3 hit single, "Hold Me, Thrill Me, Kiss Me", which was first covered in 1965 by Mel Carter (and which remains a staple of easy listening and oldies radio to this day) and later in 1994 by Gloria Estefan. She died in relative obscurity in 1985.
> - imdb.com

Wilbur Evans played our Emile, and I was totally in love with him. He had a voice that could melt your toenails. (The things my mother would say...like "a snail at full gallop.") I watched every performance. I couldn't stand not to be there when he sang "some enchanted evening" and ooooh, his voice. If he'd been around, he would have sang the "Phantom [of the Opera]." He was what a woman would dream about: a manly man, who would come in and say, "I'm here to rescue you," and then go into a song. Your heart might leap out of your chest.

Wilbur Evans, with a voice that "would melt your toenails," sang the lead, Emile, in *South Pacific*. He began opposite Mary Martin, who had to leave for a job in the United States. She was replaced by Julie Wilson.

Wilbur "Wib" Evans [August 5, 1905 – May 31, 1987] was an American actor and singer who performed on the radio, in opera, on Broadway, in films, and in early live television. He performed concerts in nearly every state and Canada. In 1951, Evans co-starred with Mary Martin in the original London production of *South Pacific*. He performed in operettas and musicals, touring extensively throughout the 1950s and '60s. Evans died at his home in Mullica Hill, New Jersey, at the age of 81.
- imdb.com

Mary Martin left the show pretty soon after I joined to return to New York to rehearse for a new Broadway show, *Kind Sir*,

Carole Leslie, left, also won a part in *South Pacific* the day Jasmine did. The two became fast friends.

and Julie Wilson replaced her. Julie, Mary Martin, Carole Leslie, and I rehearsed together. I didn't get to know Mary that well because we only rehearsed together for a short time, but she was very nice to me. "I hope you enjoy the show. Unfortunately I won't be here," she said.

Mary Martin left *South Pacific* to play Peter in *Peter Pan*, earning a Tony Award for her performance.

Mary Virginia Martin [December 1, 1913 – November 3, 199] was born in Weatherford, Texas. She was an actress, singer, and Broadway star. A muse of Rodgers and Hammerstein, she originated many leading roles over her career, including Nellie Forbush in *South Pacific* and Maria von Trapp in *The Sound of Music*. She earned Tony Awards for *South Pacific*, *Peter Pan*, and *The Sound of Music* and was nominated for Leading Actress in *I Do! I Do!* She died a month before her 77th birthday from colorectal cancer at her home in Rancho Mirage, California on November 3, 1990. - imdb.com

Julie Wilson, left with Jasmine and her two daughters, took Mary Martin's place in *South Pacific* during Jasmine's time in the show.

Julie May Wilson [(October 21, 1924 – April 5, 2015] was a singer and actress from Omaha, Nebraska, often referred to as the "Queen of Cabaret." She was nominated for the Tony Award for Best Featured Actress in a Musical in 1989 for her performance in *Legs Diamond*. She died of a stroke in Manhattan at the age of 90. - nytimes.com

Mary Martin's son, Larry Hagman, you wouldn't have looked at him twice. He was not in the show when I was. He was in the U.S. Air Force then. He had very, very bad eyesight. He was very thin. His glasses were so heavy, they looked like the bottom of Coke bottles on his eyes. He'd stand at the stage door and say, "I'm Mary Martin's son, would you like a date with me?" We'd say, "No thanks." Larry Hagman was raised in Texas while Mary Martin worked. After his Air Force duties, he stayed in England for awhile. He met and married a girl of Scandinavian background, Maj Axelsson.

Marty Martin's son, Larry Hagman, played in *South Pacific* for a short time. He went on to *Dallas* television fame.

Larry Martin Hagman [September 21, 1931 – November 23, 2012] was an American film and television actor, director, and producer best known for playing ruthless oil baron J. R. Ewing in the 1980s primetime television soap opera *Dallas*, and befuddled astronaut Major Anthony "Tony" Nelson in the 1960s sitcom, *I Dream of Jeannie*. Hagman was the son of actress Mary Martin. He underwent a life-saving liver transplant in 1995. He died on November 23, 2012, from complications of acute myeloid leukemia. – imdb.com

Our producer Jerome Whyte was a bit of a naughty boy, but everybody liked him. He was a very good producer. That first Christmas he came back to us from New York, where he had been directing something here in the U.S., we had a big Christmas party. He gave us all packages of three things in a row, rolled up—it was ladies underpants. I don't know if there was a meaning to the colors he chose; there probably was. I got one pink, one white, and one red. Did he think there was a touch of naughtiness in me? I was 17 years old. June Charlier got all red. We teased her saying, "He knows you very well." She turned red and was somewhat flustered by our teasing.

Jasmine arrives at the theater during her time in *South Pacific*. It was during this time that she met her future husband.

Composer Richard Rodgers [1902 – 1979] and lyricist Oscar Hammerstein [1895 – 1960] have been called the greatest musical theater-writing team of the 20th Century. Their work was influential, innovative and successful. They created a string of popular Broadway musicals in the 1940s and 1950s, initiating what is considered the "Golden Age" of musical theatre. Five of their Broadway shows, *Oklahoma!*, *Carousel*, *South Pacific*, *The King and I* and *The Sound of Music*, were outstanding successes, as was their television broadcast of *Cinderella*. For their adaptation of *South Pacific* from James A. Michener's book *Tales of the South Pacific*, Rodgers and Hammerstein, along with co-writer Joshua Logan, won the Pulitzer Prize for Drama in 1950. Most of their shows have received frequent revivals around the world, both professional and amateur. Among the many accolades their shows [and film versions] garnered were 34 Tony Awards, 15 Academy Awards, the Pulitzer Prize, and two Grammy Awards. - rnh.com

Richard Rodgers and Oscar Hammerstein single-handedly ushered in the "Golden Age of Musical Theater." Jasmine, with the rest of the cast, met the superstars at a Christmas party and enjoyed a song that Rodgers played for them on the piano.

Richard Rodgers and Oscar Hammerstein were both at our cast's Christmas party and each gave each cast member a bottle of champagne. They told us how happy they were that we were working there for them. Hammerstein said, "I'm so pleased to meet you all. I don't often get to meet the new people in the show. I think our cast is the cream of the crop." We were all so flattered. They were wonderful, so genuine. Richard Rodgers played the piano for us, which was a big thing and he was terrific. It was the first and only time I met them. I wish we had all had tape recorders. He played one or two pieces from the show. And several other pieces of his own. He had one little song that ended with "Merry Christmas to you," nodding his head back and forth, left and right.

Oscar Hammerstein was already suffering from cancer. He was like Smokey the Bear, big and burly, but very genteel. I was so impressed by both of them, how nice they were to the cast, very kind. I would have loved to meet them again.

The King and Queen came to see *South Pacific*. At the end of the show, before they went back to the palace, they came down from their special box and were introduced to the entire cast. We were all on the stage. First the leads were announced and they curtsied and bowed. The Queen talked to the leads. The King smiled and nodded to everyone he passed down the line, but didn't talk to anybody.

We had rehearsed before this happened. We were told that, when they came to us, not to look in their face; this was to show respect. The women were to make a deep curtsy, almost to the floor, and the men were to make a deep bow and not raise their eyes until they were back up.

Security around them at that time was really quite tight, although nobody followed them across the stage. There were all

On January 31, 1952, King George VI, right, visited *South Pacific*, with his wife Queen Elizabeth I and their daughter Princess Margaret, center. Jasmine recalled that the king looked thin and pale, and he died a short time later.

kinds of people standing in the wings. But I felt very secure, we were not in any danger and neither were they.

They were close enough that I could have touched them, not even an arm's length away. It was the King, Queen, and Princess Margaret. The Princess was a pretty girl. I remember the perfume. It smelled heavenly as they went by. It's funny the things that come back to you, I hadn't thought of it in all these years. I think even the King had on a cologne. Each one was different, probably Dior or something like that. Because we had to keep our eyes down, I saw their shoes. The Queen had very small feet. I can't tell you any more than that.

I remember the King was very thin; this was shortly before he died. He looked very sick and ashen, kind of yellow. That night he was very gaunt. Queen Elizabeth was crowned sovereign of the British Isles in 1953, shortly after her father had died.

It was unusual for a cast to be as friendly with each other as we were. Usually people are trying to compete and can be really bitchy. But we all liked each other. If somebody from our cast moved to another play or movie, we'd try to go see it and make them well aware that we were in the audience. If one of the cast was dating someone and it looked promising, we'd all get excited. If it fizzled, we'd all sympathize with her, saying that he was an idiot.

The first time I went back to London after I left the company and married Mel, my friends June and Carole arranged for a lot of the cast members still living in London at the time to get together. They called everybody and said, "Let's get together and have lunch." They managed to get this one and that one, and we ended up taking over an English public house. You can also go in for tea. It's like a bar only much nicer. It's a place where children are allowed in the gardens, but not in the area where alcohol is served. A lot of business people meet there to eat, sign a contract, or play darts. It's not rowdy, always friendly; not a gambling place. We were a bunch of ladies and our visit lasted through the lunch hour. We were so noisy we drove everybody else out. I didn't realize how noisy until I went out and came back in. I thought, "No wonder people are leaving." The cast was so pleased to be together again. It was such fun. We hadn't seen each other in a whole year. We'd been writing, but this was the excitement of seeing each other. It brought back such memories. No wonder we were so noisy.

A lot of people seemed shocked about the reunion. Casts didn't often have them, although they are having them more now. We had become a family. Julie Andrews started having them with her shows,

Ten members of the *South Pacific* cast who performed together when Jasmine was there reunited at a luncheon in London a few years later, one of the first of several cast reunions. Jasmine is pictured at center.

but until then nobody else did. In fact I think we were one of the first. But we had worked together for 18 months, every night. Some people said they were surprised we could still stand each other, but we genuinely liked each other. We were like brothers and sisters.

When Mel and I went back to London most recently, within the last 10 years, there was a new *South Pacific* on. That cast found we were having a reunion and were interested. They invited us to see their show. They had seats for us, and the manager introduced us to the audience. An interesting thing happened. One man was sitting near me with his wife, and he jumped to his feet and said, "I saw you and I remember you. I was on my honeymoon in London. I'd been married just two days. We were sitting three rows back. You looked down at us and smiled and seemed like you knew us."

I said, "You can't possibly remember me." He argued, "I do, I remember you."

Melvin looked at me and said, "Do you think he could?" I'm not sure, but he was insistent that he did.

The show was good. We visited with the cast. We thought the chorus boys were good, but they didn't have the energy as ours did when they sang, "There is nothing like a dame." The new leading man was good, had a pleasant voice, but to me Wilbur Evans will always be Emile. The girl who played the lead was also good, but there were some different scenarios. I was disappointed in Bloody Mary. I felt she had it in her, so maybe it was just an off night. Everyone else was good in their roles. Overall the play was good.

Years later, *South Pacific* was on television and everybody wanted to know what I thought of it. Glenn Close played Nellie Forbush, the female role. Producers rearranged *South Pacific*, added a couple of songs. She has a very good voice, but not as good as the cast in ours. I didn't like the changes; it was too much of it for my taste. Our Emile, played by Wilbur Evans, would make your toenails curl when he sang. Having heard him, no one else could hold a candle. Thirty percent of the dialogue was different.

PART II: PERFORMER

Chapter 18

I met Melvin while I was in *South Pacific* through a show biz friend of mine, but before that I met a U.S. Marine, whose name was George. He came to see the Latin Quarter show. He sent a note backstage at intermission, but I thought it was meant for somebody else, and passed it to several of the girls. He described me as "the second girl on the left" in this one particular dance. We saw it from the other point of view.

So anyway, George was waiting at the stage door when I came out. He mentioned a mutual friend, who was in another show. He said, "I want to introduce myself, and I'd like a date."

I responded with, "I'm not dating anyone right now."

He was stationed at a base a little ways out from the heart of London. He said, "Well, right now I

In the late 1940s and early '50s, Jasmine performed in several London stage shows. She learned how to thwart advances from fans at the stage door.

have to catch the train, but I'll be back tomorrow."

I said, "Suit yourself."

The next night he was in the front row, and he came three or four more times. I finally gave up and went out with him. We dated five or six months.

He proposed to me. I said, "George, you're a very nice man, but I'm not ready to marry anyone." I think he was from Grand Rapids, Michigan. He was only 18 and I was 16. I said, "We're both far too young." He wouldn't give up and we saw each other on and off for awhile after that.

He said, "I've written to my folks."

"I regard us as friends but I don't think we're grown up enough for marriage," I told him. He said I had broken his heart. I think I was like the prize at a shooting gallery. I really liked George. I grew really fond of him, it was like the big brother I didn't have, but not marriage material. I felt he would protect me. I didn't care if he paid or I paid on dates. I think it was like when people don't have a father image, they get attached easily. So we broke up, although he was not happy about it.

There was an English man I met through a friend. He was older than me by 10 or 15 years. I was his first show business date and he liked taking me around, "This is my girlfriend, she's doing this show or that show," he would say. He took me to some very nice places.

My mother asked, "Has he ever tried to be funny with you?"

"No."

She said, "If he does let me know." I assured her, "I'll do more than that." I couldn't tell you his name now. We dated a few more times before we finally left off. I don't think either were ever romantic. I think he just liked dating someone in show business.

There were two or three other occasions when marriage

popped up, but it wasn't to be. I guess I wasn't meant to get married before Melvin. I wasn't serious with anybody except that boy when I was 11. I hated letting these boys down, but I was far too young. I had to take care of my sister; maybe that made me seem more mature. Most people thought I was reliable. I don't pass on secrets. I'm a person who is a secret-keeper and Melvin has always respected me for that. I think most people have seen me as a more mature person than I was. When I was 12 or 13, I didn't have those giggly, silly moments. I kind of missed out on those. I was responsible for my younger sister and helping in the house. I did grocery shopping, even though I didn't know what two and two were, I usually came home with the right amount of change, though not always. I think some people think I'm stern or rigid, but I really have a nutty sense of humor and it periodically pops up.

People generalize and think show business is so shallow. You're reading from a script, so people don't think it's real. But you understand each other because you work together. So there are real, genuine relationships. But most people in show business don't marry each other; they have too much in common. Marriage is such a commitment. If you give each other your lives, you'd better have a commitment.

By this time, some of my friends had already started to be in the movies, and I realized there was good pay there. Before *South Pacific*, I had worked as an extra in a Warner Brothers movie called *Where's Charley?* that starred Ray Bolger and it came out in 1952. The British version is called, *Charley's Aunt*. It was a tough job, but it paid well. I had to be at the studio at 6:00 a.m. and it was a two-and-a-half-hour train ride from where I lived. I can't remember which of the suburbs around London the film studios were in, but it required quite a bit of travel by bus and train to get there.

In the movie, Ray Bolger arrived on the scene in a limousine with great production and disguised as a woman, all dressed up and wearing a fluffy hat. There were about 150 of us extras on a hill. The choreographer kept telling me I had moved. I said, "No, I didn't." In one of my scenes, I was running down that hill and twice I tripped, rolled down, and had to start over. The grass was wet and I had on leather soled shoes. I wore a sweet little pale blue hat, which kept trying to come off, and a pale blue suit with a blouse and a large cameo brooch. We spent a lot of time waiting to change the set while they decided what angle to film from, above or below or sideways. We spent the whole day on that one scene and they kept changing my position on the hill. It was hot, very hot. The sun was broiling. I was asked to remain for the dance scene, and had about 5 days work on that set. I can't remember what I wore in the ballroom. It seems like it was a soft pastel gown, something lovely. I remember the lovely set, with chandeliers hanging down. When I went to see it at the movies, I had to sit through it three times to make sure that was me. Because of the Technicolor, my hair turned out bright red; my natural color was actually mousy brown.

I was coming to a place in my career where I'd be having to make choices. The travel was getting to me. I was about 19 and I needed more stability in my work. I felt myself to be at a crossroad and wondered which direction I should go.

My take on my first meeting with Melvin was different from his. He was serving in the U.S. Air Force, stationed at Lakenheath Air Force Base. He came over to London sometimes on weekends. Mutual friends set us up on a blind date.

One of the first things I noticed was that he was soaking wet. Melvin had been boating on the River Thames with some friends and seaweed got stuck in the rudder. They had to dive in to free the boat.

This made him late and caused him to show up for his blind date drenched and miserable.

Jasmine and her soon-to-be husband Melvin Moran relax in London's Hyde Park. Their meeting was a blind date, which Jasmine recalls was far from successful— although she did agree to see him again.

He drove me to Winfield House, the beautiful home Woolworth heiress Barbara Hutton donated for an officers' club. It was where he was staying and he needed to change clothes before dinner. As we drove up in front of the club, I saw a man on a telephone through the windows and remembered promising to call my friend Carole Jeffries to report on my blind date. As Melvin went upstairs to change, I found my way to the room with the phones and called Carole to tell her all that had happened so far. As very few girls went on blind dates in my time, Carole was very curious. I told her we were going to have dinner in this beautiful place and some musical entertainment.

I was in a room with a sofa and a desk with a phone. While I was talking on the phone, another door opened and I saw men coming out zipping their pants. I said to Carole, "I'm not talking any more. I don't know what's going on around me, but a number of people are coming out this door zipping their pants." I came out of the room and everyone stopped and looked at me. I tried to maintain my dignity. There wasn't a movement in the room. I turned to see why everyone was so curious and saw the word "Gentlemen's" in lights over the door

I'd just come through. Boy, was I ever embarrassed. I moved to the sofa and sat down with as much aplomb as possible until Melvin returned.

We went on to dinner, where we ordered steak. When it came, it was huge. I had never seen one so big. I came from war-torn England. We could have two ounces of meat per person per week. Everything was rationed and here was this enormous steak on my plate. I cut off a piece and took it home to my family. I didn't tell Melvin what had happened with the men's room until a long time later. I felt that was best left unsaid.

The blind date did not go well from the beginning and I was uncomfortable most of the rest of the evening. He didn't talk and I couldn't stop. He gave one-word answers. It turned out he was sick, probably caught something swimming in the Thames. He threw up everything he had eaten on the way home.

But he asked me out again and I said "yes," I have no idea why. I guess it was just ordained by God. Afterwards, I went to visit my mom, who was in the hospital at the time. She asked about my date and I said it was dreadful. I'd embarrassed myself by going into the men's room without realizing it. I told her about Melvin hardly talking and then getting sick. But yet I had accepted another date with him. Mother thought I was a nut. She said, "You don't have to see him again if you don't want to."

I said, "Too late."

After a few dates, Melvin wanted to meet my family so we arranged to have a picnic. Melvin was going to pick us up and drive us to the park. My mother was so against alcohol and someone had spilled wine in the back seat of Melvin's car. He spent days driving with the window open to air it out and developed a stiff neck from the cool air. When she met him, Mother's line was, "He's a very nice young man, but have you noticed he's very badly deformed?" My mother had this Scottish sense of humor that is really weird, and if you put Scottish and English together, it's a dreadful combination.

My time with Melvin before we were married was very limited. We went out to Winfield House, dinner and dancing usually with other couples or my family, but rarely alone. Melvin was an awful dancer, the worst I ever met. Some people just can't dance. But I always say, "How would people in the theater ever have an audience if everybody danced and sang?" So I overlooked it and tried to lead him when we danced.

The first year Melvin was dating Jasmine, he bought gifts for all her family from the base commissary: toilet paper, canned turkey and bars of hand soap. Above, Jasmine's family, Michael and Lilian Geselle with Davina, right, and Helen, front, open their gifts.

Christmas came and Mel gave all my family gifts from the commissary. He brought mostly food for my mother and stepfather, enough for about a month, things we had never seen

London's Thames River figured prominently in Jasmine and Melvin's courtship. The day they met, Melvin had been boating on the Thames and fell ill on their first date.

in our lives: turkey in a can, cans of lima beans, rolls and rolls of toilet tissue and Kleenex, bars of hand soap. My sister Helen got a lovely necklace. For me, he bought a heater for my bedroom. Nobody's bedroom was heated in England. But my room was cold, so he bought me a heater. It was a strange gift to give a girl. I didn't know whether to be insulted or flattered, but it warmed the room so I was grateful.

Melvin was a nice man. He liked me because he knew I was a good woman. He was kind and fun. He proposed over New Year's Eve. We'd been going together almost a year, and I was surprised. I said, "Gee whiz, I didn't know." I don't know if we'd actually been romantic. I remember holding hands.

There were people going to bed five minutes after meeting. I didn't condemn them for it. Everybody was trying to recover from the war. Everything had changed and we didn't know what we were going to be doing day to day. War-torn Europe was a very different place than today. Morals changed a lot, I think. It's your choice, but I think there should be some responsibility to get to know each other a little bit before going to bed.

Men had been sent away to war and many didn't come back. Times were changing. You loved him and wanted him to know before he left. Everyone has their own moral code.

I always told my children that when you really love somebody you will respect them, too. Love is not just a word. Don't do something that will hurt them. I've hurt a lot of people without really knowing it. I was mature, but not about love. I appeared older than I was.

I had never met any other guy's parents. Melvin's parents had been to Europe and stopped in England a few days. I liked Melvin's father, Meyer, but he was a business man. You could barely have conversation and he was moving on. His mother, Elsie, was much more gentle and understanding, much more Melvin's nature. Although he has a lot of his father in him, especially now, running here and running there, like a chicken with its head off. I was really, really fond of his mother. She would try to help every situation, such a sweet woman. I liked her so much. It's probably why I married Melvin. She was a person I felt I could be friends with. Her personality was so gentle and kind.

I knew that if Melvin and I were to marry, we had a lot of obstacles to overcome. He thought his being Jewish might be a problem for me, but it really wasn't. I had many girlfriends who were Jewish. I was Church of England. It was impossible to go to church while touring in a show, because you would have been in a different church every week. You can talk to God in many ways, and I had never been so pious that I had to be there in church. Melvin was religious, but not overly so.

Jasmine and Melvin stroll the streets of London during their year of courtship. When it came time to decide if she wanted to be an American wife or a British actress, Jasmine hesitated, but was won over by Melvin's charm.

Many who live in Israel are very, very religious and look down their noses at others who are not of their religion. Then there are those like Melvin who believe in their religion and try to live it every day and in every way. It is very meaningful to him. He tries to help people and sometimes they don't even know. I think he kind of won me over because he is able to do these things. He shows such kindness. He will always be the first to pick up the bill, and it's because he wants to pay. He is very generous. It's the best thing about him really, his kindness and generosity. He wouldn't see evil in anybody. He really doesn't see evil and there are times when I could strangle him for that. I'll say, "They said it and they meant it."

He will say, "No, they didn't." He will say that I am a little quicker to judge than he is.

Being in the theater taught me to read body movement and character. When somebody is walking across the room, I can almost read their character. If you really take your career seriously, you can tell about people from their movements. Unfortunately, that also makes me suspicious. So marriage was a difficult decision for me. It was not easy to make that choice. In the theater, so much is based on trust. It's so important to have trust. You are committed to the show and you need to stay with it until its finished. You have to trust the other characters in your show to do what they are supposed to do when they are supposed to do it.

I was in love with Melvin, but I didn't know if I loved him enough to change my entire life. Should I stay in theater or hope to get into movies? I had done some broadcasting, but I didn't have any real credentials. I looked at some of my friends who had been married and divorced. Did I really want to spend my life with somebody and be a loving wife, or continue on trying to make it in show business? I realized I had to choose.

My mother asked, "He's a nice young man and he's very fond of you. Do you love him?"

I said, "Yes."

She said, "Enough to leave home?"

I replied, "I think so."

"Let me tell you, if I were you, I'd marry him," she said.

I asked Melvin to remain in England, but he said his whole life was oil and he didn't think he could make a living in England. We talked over several days and then I told him "yes." And if we were going to raise a family, we thought it might be important for me to convert to Judaism, so the children wouldn't be pulled back and forth.

Jasmine's mother encouraged her to marry Melvin, saying, "If I were you, I'd marry him." At the boarding house where Melvin stayed while stationed in England, with Jasmine's mother, left, and Jasmine, right.

I decided to go with Mel and hope our marriage would be a good one, and that my coming to America would be good and not a misstep. I could always go back. A lot of people came to America after World War II, but marriages were not always successful. It was a big decision. And you really don't know when you're 19 years old.

So I chose marriage and family, though I still did a bit of acting and singing after I moved to the U.S. What did I get out of show business? I got my life. I didn't think I was good enough,

Jasmine with her mother, Lilian, sister Helen and her husband Laurie, and sister Davina at Norfolk Broads in October, 1952. Melvin left England in June, 1953, and Jasmine followed in October.

nobody ever used the word, but I thought I was never going to make it. Show business builds your character, your self-confidence. I don't know what I would have done without all that experience.

PART III: WIFE, MOTHER, PHILANTHROPIST

Chapter 19

Melvin left London in June, 1953, and I followed in October. I spent those months studying for my conversion to Judaism and fulfilling my contract in *South Pacific*. When the show closed in London, I was able to get out of my contract to tour with the cast.

Mother booked me on the SS *Italia*, in a cabin with another lady. I had brought everything I owned and came alone to a place I'd never been before. It was scary. There was a hurricane at sea, and the seven- or eight-day trip turned into 10. I was seasick from the second day. There were terrific winds. Our ship tipped from side to side like in the movie *Poseidon*, and took on water. You could almost see the underside of the boat. Many of the passengers were seasick. I lost nine pounds in 10 days. I had weighed about 80 pounds when I left England. There was supposed to be one lady in my cabin, but without knowing it, I had been transferred to a slightly larger cabin. There were three other women in there and they were all seasick, the smell was awful. I hung out on the deck whenever possible, where I could get to a restroom and breathe fresh air. It was very cold and the deck was always wet. Even the captain was seasick. I was so glad to see New York.

After we disembarked, the customs agent asked if I had anything to declare. I said, "Only my wedding dress." He asked me if it had ever been worn and was nodding his head. I was so naïve. I couldn't believe anyone would ask such a question. "Of course it has never been worn," I replied.

Then he said, "I need you to tell me it has been worn or I will have to charge you 100 percent in taxes." Apparently French lace was 100 percent taxable. He was trying to help me.

Mr. and Mrs. Michael Geselle
request the honour of your presence
at the marriage of their daughter
Ruth Jasmine Lindsay
to
Mr. Melvin Robert Moran
Sunday, the twenty-second of November
at six o'clock
B'Nai Emunah Synagogue
Tulsa, Oklahoma
Reception
at half after seven
Meadowbrook Country Club

An invitation to Melvin and Jasmine's wedding was a coveted prize. Not receiving one didn't stop many of those who attended.

It took awhile before I understood and said, "Yes, it has been worn."

He promptly laughed and said, "Okay."

I felt like such a dope.

I had no idea that Melvin was relatively well off financially. Customs wanted to know who was sponsoring me. This was 55 years ago, before we had illegal aliens. His dad had to state on the forms about his finances and it was then that I realized they were a well-to-do family. I was pleasantly surprised.

Melvin met me in New York. We stayed with his cousin, Norma Pimsler, and her husband Alvin, in Great Neck, for me to ready myself for the long car ride to Oklahoma. Alvin was an artist, drawing men's clothing for top magazines and he was very good at it. Melvin had bought a new Pontiac and we drove it on the long road trip to Tulsa.

When I married Melvin, my entire family consisted of my mother, sisters, and myself. My parents were both only children. I was amazed at the number of people in Melvin's family. He had about 30 relatives living in Tulsa and other Oklahoma towns. Finally meeting everyone was quite a surprise. I thought they were the kissiest bunch I had ever met. I was sure I'd have chapped lips before I was done. Everyone was so friendly and kind. My mother-in-law planned the wedding and did a great job of it. My father-in-law paid for it because I was unable to pay for such an extravagant affair. My only guest was my mother who was able to attend because her boss gave her time off. The rest of my family could not afford the fare or time away from work.

Melvin and Jasmine with their wedding cake. Jasmine's size three wedding dress was handmade by her mother's friend from French lace.

We were married in the B'nai Emmunah Synagogue in Tulsa on November 22, 1953. My dress, a size three, was made by my mother's dear friend, who was a seamstress. The gown was of purest white and had a collar that stood up against my neck, long sleeves that came to a point, tiny pearl buttons to the waist, and a lovely chapel-length train. Melvin stepped on the skirt in the first dance and tore the hemline. It was so destroyed, I had to shorten the dress, in the hope that I could use it as a cocktail dress for special occasions. But somehow I never used it again.

There were 450 people at the wedding, and many had not been invited. They thought their invitations had been lost in the mail so they

The bridal couple are joined here by his parents, Meyer and Elsie, on the left, and her mother, Lilian, on the right. Although Jasmine's mother and two sisters were her only family, she soon learned that she was being adopted by "the kissiest bunch" of relatives ever.

came anyway. The extra folks were people who knew my father-in-law, from the early years mostly. They loved him and wanted to honor his oldest son's marriage. It was a sit-down meal at the country club and they kept putting up tables. They managed to feed everyone, but there was not a crumb of my wedding cake left for our first anniversary celebration.

We spent our wedding night at the Skirvin Hotel in Oklahoma City. While checking in at the hotel registration desk, Melvin signed simply, "Melvin Moran." We were halfway to the elevator when he stopped and looked so peculiar. I asked him if he'd forgotten something. He returned and added, "and Mrs." I remember him returning to my side with a red face. I didn't know what had happened until he told me later.

On our honeymoon, we drove to the Grand Canyon and then on to Las Vegas, Nevada, and then to California. That first morning in Las Vegas, Melvin got up early and went downstairs. He left a note joking that he had gone to win money for our breakfast. When I awoke, I read his note. I thought I'd married a Chicago gambler, like in the 1920 movies, a "Mugsie" Moran. I locked him out of the room and started to pack to fly home to Mother. He banged on the locked door while I was packing and said, "Jas, let me in."

I said, "No, I'm not going to stay married to a gambler."

He continued to bang on the door, saying, "Let me explain." After much conversation, a man's voice in another room said, "Lady, please let him in so I can go back to sleep." Mel said, "Let's go down and eat breakfast and we can talk this out." So we did and made up.

PART III: WIFE, MOTHER, PHILANTHROPIST

Chapter 20

We returned from California and settled into everyday life in Seminole, where my father-in-law wanted Melvin to learn the oil business from the ground up. The year was 1953. I had left my family behind, didn't know when I'd see them again. I left my religion, and career, to come to a whole new world. People asked strange questions. "Where are you from?" I'd say England and they'd say, "You speak very good English." This puzzled me. I couldn't believe people would think I would speak any other language.

Newlyweds Jasmine and Melvin gaze lovingly at each other. They returned from their honeymoon to make their home in small town Seminole, Oklahoma.

Moving to Seminole was a culture shock. I thought it would be like Hornchurch, but it was much smaller. The town was so clean and neat. The store windows were so spic and span. The shop owners swept the sidewalks daily. It was almost pristine.

At first I saw a lot of bias. Most people were kind, but a few were not so kind. I guess that's the same wherever you go. On one occasion I heard a man who was accompanying children say a very derogatory thing about Native Americans. I was appalled that this man, who I thought was of a certain stature, was of such low class. After a World War, it was hard to believe anyone would say such an unkind thing. It sure bothered me. More than once I just blew my stack. I would confront them and say, "How dare you say that?" I almost threw my coffee in the face of one person. He just walked away, but I was so angry I was made speechless by such a terrible thought. I confronted a few people and most hadn't even realized what hurtful

Jasmine and Melvin at the wedding of his cousin, Ethyl Landa Zale, in Tulsa a couple of years after their own wedding. The Morans' occasional trips to the big city for social events made Jasmine's transition to small-town life easier.

things they were saying. Some said they just grew up that way, had heard their family talking like this. Some got mad at me and said, "I'm not like that." When I pointed out that they were, then they'd realize maybe they were. I hoped I made them think twice before speaking this way again. I guess I will never know. We were Jewish; they were probably looking down their noses at me, too. I was certainly different.

During my first months in Seminole there was this constant heat. It was 110 or 112 degrees every day for two months, August and September. You could fry an egg on a sidewalk and people did. This was not the kind of heat we had at home. It was unbelievable to me.

I was already pregnant, sick and miserable. I cried myself to sleep every night because of the stifling heat, the backbreaking household tasks, long before most people had dishwashers and microwave ovens. I tried hard to adapt to life as a married woman, but the homesickness was devastating.

I missed English cooking. It took a long time to get used to the food. The items in the grocery store weren't the same. I couldn't find bread like I was used to. The bread here was so gooey, but it was about all you could buy if you couldn't get Jewish or rye bread, which wasn't sold in Seminole at that time. We bought Jewish rye bread when we went to Tulsa and kept it in the freezer. My mother, when she came, called Wonder Bread "guck." We were used to French and German bread. It also took a long time to get used to tea bags. Tea was never in a bag where I grew up.

There were some good places to eat in Seminole. Daisy's Drive-in made wonderful hamburgers. Unfortunately they added mustard or mayonnaise, which I hated. As long as they left it off, I was a happy camper. There was the Waffle House; I didn't know what a waffle was. It was owned by Jimmie Angel and his cousin Gus Eugenious. They were Greek. The Waffle House was next to where

First National Bank used to be. The waffles were very good. I really enjoyed the occasional meal there. They also had wonderful stews and soups.

There were at least three theaters, maybe more, including a drive-in on the edge of town. We went to the movies at least once a week. Our Jewish ladies formed a card club and we played Canasta at least once a week, not for high stakes. The most you could win was 75 cents and you had to be very good to win that. I'm not sure I ever won that much. I won 50 cents a number of times. It was fun and there was much fun and camaraderie. Melvin liked to play gin rummy, and he was good at it. He was good at all card games, but poker was gambling and I wasn't brought up with it. It rubbed me the wrong way when he played poker.

I'd seen too much gambling in movies. This was before TV. I thought it encouraged gangsterism. It was a bone of contention for a short period.

Seminole had its dangerous side then. It seemed like the movie *Chicago*. Despite prohibition-type laws, if you wanted alcohol, you just called a cab and it would be delivered to you. It was bootlegged. I had only heard the word from the old movies. Boy, did I learn in a hurry. Drink was everywhere. I didn't know what the big deal was, but Oklahoma was a dry state. Bootlegging involved a lot of gang-style action. We could write a whole book about that activity. Both Melvin and I decided we didn't like what we saw in Seminole.

Melvin was called to serve on a grand jury investigating the corruption of local law enforcement, some lawyers and bootleggers. The grand jury was sequestered in a hotel in Wewoka, and not allowed to come home during the time of the hearings. I had phone calls at night saying that if my husband didn't vote the right way, they'd kill him or hurt me. I am 19 years old, just arrived from England, but I had seen the movies. I would barricade myself in my house, put chairs under the door knobs. My husband was gone and I was all alone. I didn't know if somebody was going to come and shoot me in the middle of night or what.

If not for our nice neighbors, I would have gone home. We lived at 717 McKinley. Charles and Wanda Sims lived on one side. They were sweet and kind and had a little girl and a boy. Charles Sims was an attorney, the son of Seminole's infamous police chief Jake Sims.

On the other side was a lovely couple, Tug and Mary Barber, with two of the sweetest little girls. The houses were very close to each other. The Barbers' bedroom window was right next to ours. If we left ours open at night, they could hear everything. Most people didn't leave windows open that close, they'd just use the fan in the ceiling and the window on the other side. I told Mary about the phone calls. I was really worried. She said, "Don't just lay there and worry. Leave the window open and scream like the devil and Tug will be over like a bullet from a gun."

I did leave the window open and felt much more comfortable. It seemed like the grand jury investigation went on for an eternity, but maybe it was only one month. I was worried and away from home. I didn't know what to do, I was getting phone calls at night, people telling me that I was in deep trouble. I didn't know anybody and I didn't know who to trust. My mother had already taught me about danger and being aware of people. But my comfort came from knowing people like the Barbers were close at hand.

Finally indictments were returned and the grand jury was released. We settled into our life in Seminole. Melvin tried to take me to Oklahoma City or Tulsa on the weekends to the theater or for other cultural events, trying to make things as much like home as possible. But that first year was very difficult.

PART III: WIFE, MOTHER, PHILANTHROPIST

Chapter 21

Melvin had said that someday we would move to Tulsa, but for now he was running his dad's business and he was needed in Seminole. I thought I would want to live in Tulsa, but after we made friends here, and I had been born and raised in a small town, I realized I fit in a small town more easily than I would have in a big town. Of course, every time I wanted to do something we had to go a long way. But I developed a taste for Seminole. And, of course, our children were born here and we became very involved in the schools and local activities.

When it came time for Melvin's father to retire, he offered us a chance to take his office in Tulsa. But by then, I was more settled. There were a few friends that Melvin had gone to school with and sometimes we would go out to dinner with them on a Saturday night, but Seminole was my home. In Seminole, I joined organizations—the Garden Club, Parent-Teacher Association, the Chamber of Commerce, a square dancing group, a bowling league, and the Welcome Wagon. I was involved in many other activities. I was happy here.

I think God has a place for you when he breathes life into you and he drops you into a certain slot. I think I should have been dropped into the Victorian era, where children are seen and not heard and vulgarity was not tolerated. People think I am terribly judgmental, and I admit that I am often quick to judge, but that's the way God and my mother made me.

You know we are like diamonds. A cut diamond has many facets. You can see the beauty as it flashes in the light, but some of the underlying areas are not as attractive when you turn it over. I think some women look through to the souls of people. When I form an opinion, sometimes it takes years to find out why I feel that way, but I find that I am usually right.

Melvin says to me, "You're so judgmental." Melvin is the opposite; he is so trusting. And we don't always agree on people. For example, Melvin has a good relationship with this one individual. They have worked together on a few things. I say, "I hope you are not trusting him too much. The relationship seems to work for you, but I don't want to be around him."

Melvin says, "I still like him."

"Okay, that's fine."

Melvin would see him in his best light anyway. It's hard for me to be nice when I really don't like someone. I try never to be rude, but I don't go out of my way to be nice to people that I believe aren't what they should be.

Scottish tempers are well known all over the world. Melvin has been really betrayed by some people over the years. There was a local man who betrayed him at a bad time. I told Mel to be wary of him, but he didn't believe me. I believe it's because I learned to read mannerisms in my work that I can often tell a person's character by the way they move, the way they talk. I realized at an early age who my real friends are. They won't betray you. I've been hurt for Mel. On several occasions, I've told someone, "You really let my husband down at a time when he needed you." Melvin has been such a true friend to so many people.

Things I have seen in my life, in Seminole and other places, have made me much more loyal to my husband or family. For example, I never understood double timing your husband. If you fall out of love, why don't you separate and divorce, why carry on with the next door neighbor? I always thought that loyalty was more important than about anything. Couples should stick together through thick and thin. To me, loyalty may be the most important character trait there is. I'd pack my bags and walk away; I would never carry on with somebody else. I can't understand people doing that. But when I've seen it, I made up my mind that if I couldn't help, I'd say nothing. My mother always used to say, "If you can't say something nice about someone, say nothing," and I agree. My mother hated gossip, oh she hated it, she thought it the vilest thing. Here's what I say, "A little bit of gossip, embellished on its way, can make someone unhappy, can ruin someone's day." And

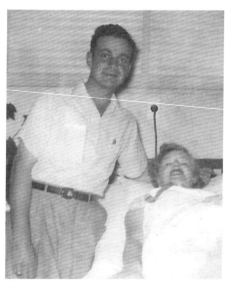

it's true. I write these things down when I read them or think of them. I have pens and papers everywhere. I always say Confucius was a very wise man.

I got pregnant right away. I was scared and excited and sick as a dog. There was the anticipation of bringing a human being into the world, being able to teach it all the important things in life. You want them to be good citizens. But I was still a young person

Melvin and Jasmine in Seminole Municipal Hospital after the birth of firstborn Marilyn. Melvin waited anxiously at home for the arrival, called afterwards by the hospital staff.

myself. Maybe I should have waited a few more years until I was more mature. It was tough, especially with our first child being so sick. If Elisa had been born first, it would have been so much easier.

Our first child, Marilyn, had a spastic colon. She couldn't drink any kind of cows' milk. After being hospitalized in Tulsa, a doctor convinced me to try goat's milk as I was unable to nurse her. And it was the answer. Our local doctor had thought I was just a nervous new mother, but after that I learned to speak up. I became a ferocious mother. Melvin said, "You're not the girl I married." Very few people remain exactly the same and I realized there were times I had to make a scene on behalf of my family.

When Elisa came along, she ate everything. She scared the daylights out of me once and I never forgot it. I liked to make fried chicken. It was not common in England. My mother-in-law taught me how; she was a really good cook. So I put this fried chicken on the table. Elisa was about five months old and she was in this baby chair that had a tray that went all around her. I turned to the stove and then when I turned back, she had a chicken leg and was chewing on the end. She already had maybe four teeth. She had gotten the flesh ripped off the chicken and some of it was going down. I tried to grab it and she was biting me. I was screaming with fear and pain. I thought it was going to strangle my daughter. We had a wrestling match but she got most of the chicken down. She really wanted that chicken. How on earth she ate it, I can't imagine.

Baby food wasn't good enough for her after that. Once she got that chicken in her mouth she wanted more tasty stuff. Melvin came home, and I told him, "She swallowed a chicken leg. I don't know if I should call the doctor or not. I was trying to get it out of her mouth. Between my blood and the chicken, she got it all down. I got the bone away from her, but she didn't leave anything on it." I was trying to do the Heimlich maneuver and she was screaming. It was one of those hellish moments one never forgets. From then on she never looked back: baby food, forget it. The strange thing is she has since become a vegetarian and does not eat meat at all.

David was always so engrossed in books. You could never get him to set them down. He learned to read at an early age, very, very early. If there was a book or newspaper on the table, don't set food down. He'd eat a whole plate of whatever was made for the whole family. I like to make salmon croquettes. That's when I realized what a voracious eater David was. He was about five and he had a book in his hand and sat down at the table. I told him we were not ready to eat yet, and he knew I didn't like him reading at the table. He said, "I'll put my book down when it's time to eat."

I put a plate of croquettes down on the table. I turned around and when I came back, the plate was empty. I asked David, "What did you do with the croquettes?"

He said, "What croquettes?"

"I put eight croquettes on the table," I told him.

He said, "Well I may have eaten one or two."

"You had eight croquettes!"

"I couldn't have," he argued. But he did. And that was a lesson for me.

I tried to teach the children a little Scottish dancing, but it was not to be. They just weren't interested and so we left that alone. Most kids want to do acrobatics, but ours really

Melvin and Jasmine Moran are pictured here with their family, Marilyn, Elisa, and David, in 1964. Their children, who have accomplished many successes, are a source of pride for the couple.

didn't. David was interested in running and ran marathons until he developed ankle trouble, which is prevalent in our family.

I followed in my mother's footsteps, singing to my children and telling them fairy stories, as I still do with my grandchildren. I think everyone should have a little magic in their lives. One of my favorites is "The Elf and the Dormouse," written in the late 1800s by Oliver Herford.

Under a toadstool crept a wee Elf
Out of the rain to shelter himself.
Under the toadstool, sound asleep,
Sat a big Dormouse all in a heap.
Trembled the wee Elf, frightened and yet
Fearing to fly away lest he get wet.
To the next shelter – maybe a mile!
Sudden the wee Elf smiled a wee smile.
Tugged till the toadstool toppled in two.
Holding it over him, gaily he flew.
Soon he was safe home, dry as could be.
Soon woke the Dormouse – "Good gracious me!
"Where is my toadstool?" loud he lamented.
— And that's how umbrellas first were invented.

The children were intense about school and math. They all loved math. It was the worst subject in the world to me. My children found school challenging and they liked to try to reach their goals. They never had any problems at school.

Once when Marilyn was about seven, she got off the bus crying. It was a hot day and she was all hot and sweaty and wet from crying.

When I asked her what was wrong, she said, "I can't tell you. You're going to be so mad."

"Well, you have to tell me."

She hemmed and hawed for about five

The Moran Family continued to grow, pictured in 1968.

minutes and kept crying. I said, "No matter what it is, it can't be as bad as you're making me think it is."

I could hardly understand her when she said, "I got a B in math."

I said, "Good Lord, if I had gotten a B in math the entire town would have cheered and my mother would have declared a holiday!" I always told our kids never to worry about grades if they had done the best they could. I'd never be mad at them because of their grades. A number doesn't mean anything in life. It's whether you tried or not.

Our children had good close friends in and out of school. It was important to me for them to integrate within the community and it pleased me that they had good friends and didn't just keep to themselves. I think it's a major problem when children don't share fun and exchange ideas. Verbal communication is very important in our world. I wish we had more today.

We did Brownies, PTA, and Girl Scouts. I got to know a lot of good people. We did debate, karate, and swimming lessons at St. Gregory's. All three of our children took swimming there. The pool in Seminole was too deep; if you couldn't touch bottom they couldn't take lessons. Therefore, I drove them to St. Gregory's in Shawnee for swim lessons three times a week. They are all good swimmers now.

Learning to eat kosher wasn't that difficult, it was just foreign to me. The word kosher means clean. Foreign substances, like the dirt on potatoes, would be removed. I still can't eat potatoes with the skin on. The eyes have dirt in them. When I peel a potato, I clean the eye out. When I bake a potato, I clean it first with a toothbrush, but I still will not eat the skin. Meat must be completely lean; we salt to make sure it is perfectly clean.

In the strictest religion, you are not supposed to eat meat and milk together. In Israel and other warmer countries, most milk came from goats. It's a lot thicker and stronger. In the early years, there was no refrigeration so eating thick goat milk and meat together can disturb the balance of the stomach. Milk spoils more easily. The laws of Kasha were meant to keep the tribe healthy and to ensure they did not die from bacterial diseases. Butter or any products of milk are not supposed to be eaten with meat. They eat meat at one meal, and may consume milk products at another.

We tried to keep a kosher home for several years, especially after Marilyn had such terrible problems with her stomach. But there was no kosher butcher in Oklahoma; our meat had to come from Kansas City packed in ice. The meat arrived in Seminole in the late afternoon and I'd go pick it up. There was no direct bus route. The package had to change buses en route. It traveled under the bus where there was no air conditioning. Once or twice, the bus didn't arrive on time and the meat spoiled, wasting maybe $100 I couldn't afford. More than once I sat at the bus station and cried over a box of reeking meat that had literally fried in the sun.

After awhile I told Melvin that this was ridiculous, we were wasting money and we couldn't go on like this. It was impossible to keep my freezer full. So we stopped buying kosher meat, though we still won't eat pork. But we do eat meat and milk together.

Christmas was a problem for awhile. I wasn't celebrating that now that I was Jewish, but we had to explain it to the children. In school, everybody came back from Christmas telling what they did or what they got. Our kids had to explain that we didn't have Christmas, we had Hanukah. Unfortunately, my mother-in-law died about two and a half years after Melvin and I were married, so she didn't get a lot of opportunity to guide me through the traditions—like at Passover when there can be no piece of bread in the house. I had to feel my way around the traditions. But Melvin's Aunt Minnie Bennett, his mother's youngest sister who lived in Seminole, helped me and explained about Passover and other Jewish holidays. Thank goodness for that. She really was a wonderful person and I missed her so much when she died about 13 years after I married Melvin.

There was a good Salvation Army here at the time. We wanted our children to learn charity, so we had them go through their toys and give some of the toys they no longer played with to Salvation Army. At that time, the firemen were good to repair toys if you had kept the parts. If a wheel fell off a little cart, they would fix it and paint it and make it like it was new again. We have so many good people here. The police take toys to needy kids. Everyday workers did nice and kind things. The teachers would take their own children's clothes to needy children in their classroom. There wasn't so much poverty then, not as obvious as it is now. Today fewer people are working and they declare it when they have a problem. At that time they just kept quiet, but you'd know when the kids came to school half dressed or wearing a dirty dress or blouse. Back then, it was what you saw instead of what you knew.

I wanted my children to speak out when they saw something wrong. I didn't want them to just sit there and say nothing, and when they could help somebody, they would. Debate gave them that ability.

We had many debate tournament weekends. There were times when I met myself coming and going, but I wanted them to have that experience. They spent time listening to other people debate. Then we sent them away to college, hopefully to grow into productive, healthy adults.

Jasmine's family continued to grow throughout the 1960s. Her mother, Lilian, and stepfather, Michael, center, pose with the families of her daughters. Back row, from left, are an unnamed couple who were friends of Helen, with Helen between them; Michael and Lilian; Jasmine; Davina; and Jasmine's husband Melvin, holding son David. Front row from left, are Helen's children, Jennifer (whom Helen is holding), Bruce, and Allison, and Jasmine's daughters, Elisa and Marilyn.

When my children grew up, moved on, and made their own traditions, I was prepared to let them make their own way. I knew it was time to release the bird from the nest. All birds must learn to fly. I learned to fly at a very early age and sometimes it felt lonely but I learned from this.

I am so proud of my children. They make their livings with their speech and personality. Marilyn works so hard and has achieved the goals she wanted to achieve. One of the men who ran for governor in Indiana and won, wanted her to be lieutenant governor. But she didn't want to give up her life, which was wise. Politics is a very hard life. She wanted to talk with Daddy and me first, but if she left her business, her husband would have to take care of it alone, and it's not something that could be done alone. It required a full-time commitment by both of them and she realized it. Their business, which started out making TV commercials for small businesses, now does in-house work for large companies, such as GE and Airstream. They teach people to learn new innovations that come into the businesses. It's hard work but, they both love it.

Marilyn and her husband, Bill Townsend, have two girls, Allison and Julie, both married and both well established in their careers. Allison is a pharmaceutical representative and married to a pediatrician, Aaron Sackett. They have a son, Nathan, and two daughters, Natalie and Kate. Julie works for Marilyn's company and is married to Panchito Townsend from Chile and they have two children, Jasmine and Francisco. Panchito is the director of the YMCA in Fort Wayne, Indiana, where all Marilyn's family lives.

Elisa was a very imaginative child. If there were any rules, she would see how far she could go. I think this is a family characteristic. Sometimes the rules aren't fair and need to change. Being this way made her imagination expand and she ended up becoming a lawyer.

She is a brilliant researcher. If she takes your case, she will go with it for years if necessary until it is completed. She is a tough little cookie, so fair and so generous. She also works very hard within the district of Denver, Colorado, trying to improve the lives of homeless children. She has started many programs to assist in giving them a future. And she works with animal rights programs as well.

Elisa and her husband, Gary Kleiman, have two daughters, Nicole and Michelle. Nikki has recently graduated with highest honors from the University of Michigan and is in law school at Colorado University. Michelle is a pediatrician and is married to Eric Shiffman, who has a master's degree in business and works in Denver. They all live in Colorado.

All our children are animal rights' activists. They would run barefoot through thorns or snow to reach an animal in trouble. Mel and I are so proud that they share their love of God's creatures with us.

David was always very introspective. He had his own little world. He could be very animated when talking about people or animals in trouble. Otherwise, he was relatively quiet and you didn't always know what he was thinking. You knew it wasn't bad thoughts, though. He read voraciously, he was never without a book. He read everything about science and was terribly interested in being a scientist.

Science was his whole life. We thought we had another Carl Sagan, he was that wrapped up in physics. The University of Michigan chased him for weeks. He had been offered other scholarships but Michigan had a good physics program. And he loved it, but he had a bad experience with a professor who didn't give him credit for work he did. It hurt David deeply.

During the summer break, David worked in Alaska battling an oil company over a causeway that kept small fish from swimming downstream. Physics taught him what would happen to the fish and the law helped him prove it. So David turned to law. He spent two years at Cambridge University in England, which he loved. He taught at Cornell University in New York state, and he has seven degrees. He eventually became a law professor at the University of Michigan and co-founded the university's Innocence Project, reopening cases where innocent people may have been wrongly convicted. He is currently the director of the University of Michigan Innocence Project. He has managed to prove that many of them did not commit the crime they are convicted of. He has appeared before the U.S. Supreme Court with six different cases and continues successfully in this field.

David and his wife, Kris, also have two daughters, Ingrid and Anika, both still in school in Ann Arbor, Michigan. Kris has a high position overseeing Michigan's clean water in area lakes.

PART III: WIFE, MOTHER, PHILANTHROPIST

Chapter 22

I was taking the kids to speech, to kung fu, to swimming, to debate, and sometimes I had the chance to perform in Oklahoma City. I was never out of the car. Melvin was working so hard. There were times when I hijacked him, just had the car packed when he came home on Friday evening and we headed off with the kids to a state park or some other place for the weekend. We always enjoyed the peace and tranquility from the stress of our lives.

As the children grew up, we went on vacations on our own and have had some wild adventures. Once we were in Acapulco for a meeting of some oil organization Mel was a member of. We were relaxing on the beach and I saw this man going into the air and just gliding through the air. Then I saw the rope attaching his sail to a Jeep. It looked so peaceful. I said to Melvin, "Doesn't that look wonderful?"

He said, "Not to me."

I said, "Melvin, you act like you're 94. Let's find out about this. It looks like fun. Imagine what you can see from up there." The Jeep came back and the man came down slowly as little boys rushed up to help pull him down.

I said, "Let's go see how much it costs."

Melvin said, "You don't want to do something like that."

The cost was reasonable, like $20, so I said, "Let's do it."

He asked, "Do you really want to?" I said I did, but he said he didn't really want to. So I talked him into it and he went first. He was almost screaming. He said he had never been so frightened in his life. His knuckles were absolutely white, his nails embedded in his palms. He is afraid of heights. I didn't know this. He was petrified.

When he came down, he said, "I can't believe you made me do that."

"Didn't you enjoy any of it?" I asked. He did not.

You're supposed to tip the young boys who help you down and Melvin tipped because he was so glad he didn't have two broken legs. But when he saw the film later, he realized they just came up after he fell down. They never touched him or helped him in any way, but he tipped them generously.

I had a wonderful time. It was beautiful and just what I expected. I could see well over the hotel. I was glad we were not over the ocean because if the rope broke, I couldn't have swam back. I took in all the beauty. The birds flying close didn't bother me, it was all so gorgeous. I was in seventh Heaven.

We were probably up 10 or 15 minutes. I saw the air start to come out of the parachute and I began to come down gracefully. The boys didn't touch me, but they ran up to get money.

Later after we came home, Dinah Shore, who used to have an afternoon TV show, was talking to a young man who had plummeted to the ground at 65 miles an hour. It was amazing he was still alive. The poor guy, his parachute collapsed and it nearly killed him. It was the same strip of beach where we were and, in his case, the wind dropped. Oh, how lucky we were that it was such a windy day and we flew beautifully.

Once when I went snorkeling, I came up between the legs of the great-granddaughter of a past governor of Grand Cayman Island. She thought I was an octopus. She was waiting for the Queen of England who was coming to visit her. I know it sounds crazy,

Jasmine turns every vacation into an adventure. From snake charming to wind surfing, her fearlessness isn't always matched by Melvin.

but this is the way of my life. Here is the story.

We were on a cruise to the Grand Cayman Islands and walking on the beach when two people asked us if we wanted to snorkel. There had been no equipment left to rent, so this couple said we could use theirs if we turned it in when it was due in two hours. They gave us a little lesson on how to use it.

We were having a ball. A pink fish with a black stripe swam right up to my nose. It looked into my eyes. I went blink, blink, blink, and it swam away. I followed it and it would stop and just wait for me, then move again. I wondered where it was taking me. There was a big piece of brain coral, half the size of a kitchen table. Little crabs were coming out of the holes in the coral. It fascinated me. The fish I had followed swam into a little nooky place and came back out as if to say, "This is my home."

I realized suddenly that I hadn't seen Melvin in a while, so I went to the surface to look for him. I had swum for miles and I couldn't see Melvin anywhere. And I realized I was in deep water a long way from the beach. I really panicked. I pulled my goggles back on and started swimming in the direction I thought was the beach. What if a shark came and nobody knew where I was? I was swimming as fast as I could when something caught my shoulders and waist and was holding me real tight and I couldn't get away. I twisted my body and arms and legs and turned over swallowing water, thinking I was probably caught by an octopus. It was then that I realized that I was nearly on dry land so I could stand up. I stood up quickly.

This poor woman was coming up, too. I had swum between her legs and brought her down. We both surfaced coughing and sputtering, trying to get our senses together and finally realized what had happened.

She had to be in her 70s and I was in my 40s. She was not dressed in a swimsuit because she hadn't been planning to go swimming. Just then two men in suits came running with guns drawn. She turned, saw them, and waved them away, explaining to me that they were her security detail. When I apologized, she said, "You're English. What are you doing here?" I introduced myself and she introduced herself. She said Queen Elizabeth was also on the island and the woman was holding a dinner for her. "Please come as my guest," she said. I told her my ship was sailing at 7:00 p.m. She said, "Don't worry, we can fix you up." I thanked her but said I couldn't. We visited for quite a while. I had soaked the woman's clothing and she was going to have her hair done again. She had already had it done earlier that day. I apologized again and she asked again if I didn't want to be their guest. I laughed and said I couldn't. She was the great-granddaughter of a past governor of the Cayman Islands and now lived in California. She was there specifically to host this event for the queen.

Apparently the Cayman Islands have played a part in British

history and that's why the Queen was there to visit. When I got back to the ship, I asked Melvin if this really happened. He said, "I don't know, I wasn't there." It was all so unreal to me, how it really happened.

> The British monarch appoints the Governor of the Cayman Islands, which belong to the United Kingdom. The role of the Governor is to act as head of state. The official residence of the Governor is Government House on Seven Mile Beach, Grand Cayman. - gov.ky

I always try to talk to people I meet in airports or when traveling. Some of my best stories and experiences come from accidental meetings. I think God puts us in a certain time or place for just that purpose. I don't remember half the tours I've taken. My best memories are from the people I meet along the way.

Once when I was in the Los Angeles airport getting ready to depart for Hawaii, I met a man and had one of the best conversations of my life. Melvin had just left me to make a phone call and he was talking and talking on the phone. The man asked me where I was off to and if I was alone. I looked at Melvin and said, "For all intents and purposes, yes." When I told him I was going to Hawaii, he asked if I had been there before. I told him no.

He said, "I was born in Hawaii and lived there almost all my life. May I give you some ideas?" Our itinerary was relatively busy, but we still had some room, so I said yes that would be nice. He had been the chief gardener at the Royal Palace Gardens and knew the island so well.

He was very animated and sweet. He suggested we go to the Ala Moana Tower, the highest on the big island, where there is a wonderful restaurant. "It is far too expensive, though," he said. "Go between 7:00 and 8:00 p.m. for cocktail hour. Do not order alcohol because it's overpriced. Just sip your drink and watch the sun go down on the ocean, it's one of the most beautiful sights you will ever see."

He also said there were two buses that would take you. "If you go in the daytime, buses run about every 15 minutes," he said. "In the evening, sometimes you will have to wait 30 or 40 minutes, but you can occupy yourself by looking at the beautiful homes in the area. They maintain their gardens so beautifully." So we followed his suggestions. The sight of the setting sun was memorable and the view was spectacular.

I've found the things you see through Mother Nature are the most beautiful, so I was interested in all he had to say. He told me what bus number to take. We did, and that sunset was one of the most beautiful experiences of my life, even though the sunsets in Oklahoma are some of the most spectacular in the world.

When we finished there, he told us to take another bus to a Hawaiian restaurant, to try the seafood. I had a list as long as your arm from him, wonderful ideas of places to go and see. I will never forget him and we followed almost all the suggestions he made. I told Melvin he missed the best experience of our trip, talking with this guy. I followed at least four of his suggestions. In the palace gardens, he said, the flowers will change colors at different times of the day. He recommended that we go back and look again in four hours and see the change in the colors of the flowers that the sun would make. He told us to stand at the bridge on the big koi pond to watch the sunset, how it shines on the water. He should have been a tour guide. His recommendations were terrific. I learn so much when I stop to visit with people. He made our trip to Hawaii most memorable.

I remember making Melvin take the helicopter over the waterfalls in Hawaii that can only be seen by air. Melvin is so afraid of heights, but I said, "Look, I've done a lot of things for you. What if we do go down? We'll be dead, you won't know." And it was some of the most gorgeous scenery in the world, which we would never have seen if we hadn't gone. Melvin enjoyed it, but he was very nervous.

I strongly suggested we take another helicopter ride in Alaska. We started on a helicopter that lands in the water. When it landed, he thought we were sinking. His eyes were closed and there were drops of sweat on his forehead. But when he realized we were on dry land, he was much relieved. I think he secretly enjoyed it, but he never admitted to it.

Melvin and Jasmine aboard the submarine *Nautilus* in Cozumel. Never content to lie on a beach, Jasmine's trips add education and history to her adventures.

PART III: WIFE, MOTHER, PHILANTHROPIST

Chapter 23

After the children started leaving home, Melvin's life took over. He became more of a political person and ran for office, and this spilled over onto me. I needed to talk to people and go to meetings. I was involved in everything in town, from the Chamber of Commerce Welcome Wagon to Garden Club to Meals on Wheels. I was often the secretary or the Ways and Means chair. Sometimes there was no way and so I was scrambling to find a means. It wasn't always easy, but I learned a lot of lessons from working with these organizations: patience, tolerance, and good will.

Together Melvin and I bowled in a league and learned square dancing, both of which we found fun and interesting. We played canasta with a Jewish group. Bridge was the popular game here at that time, but I enjoyed canasta.

We always tried to help people when we could. If I found out someone needed help, and I could visit and not be intrusive, I'd try to help with whatever it took. If they had bills running up that they couldn't pay or whatever, I tried not to be too obvious and embarrass the person. You don't want to step into someone's home and say, "Oh, you're poor." I don't want to look like Mother Theresa. It's been a

Dinner with the President

A dinner attended by Jasmine and Melvin with President John F. Kennedy on January 31, 1963, featured this program. Other attendees included senators, congressmen, and ambassadors.

blessing to me when I was able to help quietly so they didn't know who had helped them.

Melvin served on the City Council, was elected mayor twice, named Citizen of the Year, and inducted into the Seminole Hall of Fame. He was a director and later president of the Oklahoma Independent Petroleum Association and served on Oklahoma's Academy for State Goals. He was active in the Jewish organization, president of B'nai Brith, and served on the regional board for the Anti-Defamation League.

I was completely at home in Seminole by now, but the decision to become a U.S. citizen was difficult. It was hard to separate myself from my country. I left my home, my religion, and my family to come to here, but my British citizenship was still part of my identity. However, I realized it was not fair to my children, and I couldn't vote for my husband when he ran for City Council.

Of course, I said I wouldn't vote for him anyway because he wouldn't fix the road in front of our house. I scraped my bumper every time I turned into my driveway. I became a citizen when he ran the second time, but I still did not vote for him for the same reason. Until it was fixed, I would not vote for him. All my friends laughed at me, but I said, "I'm English and I stick to my guns." It was a battle of principle and nobody won.

During the 1960s, Melvin was a board member of the Oklahoma, Texas and Louisiana chapter of the Anti-Defamation League. In that capacity, we were invited to Washington, D.C. for a dinner with President John F. Kennedy on January 31, 1963, at the Sheraton-Park Hotel.

It's really a weird story. It's another time when my mother's sixth sense seemed to rear up in my own life.

We had voted for Kennedy and thought he would be good for

the country. The whole country was fascinated by the Kennedys. It was "Camelot," you know. Every time Jackie went out the door, there were 400 photographers. Mrs. Kennedy had a baby and lost another one. Everybody was in bereavement. The whole world was enamored of this young man and woman.

I was pregnant with David at the time, born four months later in May 1963. I remember the weather that winter was dreadful. The doctors didn't want me to travel, it was so icy and cold in Washington, and David was such a big baby, nearly 10 and a half pounds when he was born. I was really huge even though it was still a few months before he was due. Anyway, there were difficulties carrying him and the doctor thought I should not travel, but it was such an unusual thing, to be able to hear the President speak. Before they even sent the tickets, we had to have a profile to make sure we weren't hiding anything or have a dangerous background and we had to be fingerprinted.

I needed a new suit to wear, so I went to Ada to a maternity shop and I bought a brown maternity suit, silk, a classic cut. It was winter so I needed something warm and dressy. My own maternity clothes were not dressy enough for something like this: We were going to hear President John F. Kennedy speak so my clothing had to be special.

It was my first trip to Washington, D.C., so we saw the White House. We went to Washington's home and all the other things tourists do. We saw the national museum, the cemeteries. The whole thing was so meaningful. Washington is living history. I never walk past an exhibit, but try to learn more about it; I'm still this way today. My mother called me a nosey parker and I am. We took some tours on buses and sometimes we took a cab, so we could see something in two hours instead of the four it would ordinarily take with a tour group. I wanted to know as much as I could, but I was so big and pregnant

I could have used a wheelbarrow in front of me. We have been to Washington a number of times since, but this was the first time. But of course the first time is always exciting.

On the night of the dinner, we got into the Sheraton-Park Hotel at the appointed time and were seated as soon as possible. Our meal was served almost immediately. No food would be served after the President's arrival because his speech would be televised nationally. They didn't want any clinking silverware during the broadcast. Kennedy wasn't going to eat with us... well, maybe dessert.

But they told us we wouldn't be able to leave the room after the President arrived. If you needed to go to the ladies' room, do it after you finish the meal, but before he arrived. I was so big and pregnant and I had to go to the bathroom often. I asked Melvin what to do and he said, "Make sure you go before the President arrives." I remember worrying myself about it all through the meal. I tried not to drink very much.

They made it a very special night. Our seating was unbelievable. Many members of both the House of Representatives and Senate were there. Some of the most famous people included Henry Kissinger, who went on to serve as National Security Advisor and Secretary of State; Teddy and Robert Kennedy; and the ambassador to France, Charles Bohlen, and his wife, who was a very beautiful woman. She could have been a movie star. She was dressed so beautifully and he was, too. All the people you are familiar with were there: Jim Wright, Speaker of the House; Carl Albert; James R. Schlesinger; LBJ. Lady Bird was there, too, although her name isn't listed but she was there. Maybe she came at the last minute. Some of the wives did. It was a gilded night, that's the best way to describe it. It was truly an amazing evening.

We got into the dinner. I forget who we were seated with; they seated you with the region from which you came. It was an enormous table with just other various members of the Anti-Defamation League. I couldn't tell you who now. Soon after the meal I went to the restroom and tried to give myself enough time to return before the arrival of the President.

Before I left, I made sure I got my guest ticket from Melvin so if anything happened I could prove I was rightfully there. Melvin had to look for the ticket and then it was quite a distance to the restroom. I had thought some of the guests would go to their hotel rooms, but they all went to the ladies room. By the time I got to the restroom, there were oodles of women ahead of me. I thought I'd never get through the enormous line. I ended up being the last to get in. I hoped the President hadn't come and I'd be banging on the door saying, "Let me in." I rushed back as fast as I could, and fortunately the President had not yet arrived.

When I got back, I said, "You know, Melvin, something troubles me. You know how insistent I was to have my ticket? Nobody else was showing their tickets. Wouldn't you think security would be very tight right now? Somebody could have waylaid me in the restroom, banged me on the noggin, taken my clothes, put a pillow in there, and returned in my place."

"But I would have known," Melvin said. "They wouldn't have known what seat to take. You're seeing things again." I was more than miffed at him.

I said, "From where I am I could shoot the president, if I wanted to."

He said, "What a dreadful thought." And it was.

"I just don't like the security," I stated.

This was a dreadful thought, but on this night just 10 months before President Kennedy was assassinated, I thought how easy it would be to shoot the president. The lack of security was appalling and I was horrified because I realized how important security should have been.

Before I came to Washington, the Secret Service had almost examined my teeth, but since we got there, the security was really lax. I had a fairly large gold lame purse and could have had a revolver. Even when I came in at the start of the evening, nobody looked at my purse. They patted Melvin down. But I could have had a gun. When I went to the ladies' room, someone could have left a gun there earlier in the day, I could have put it in my purse.

Melvin said, "You have the most awful ideas. You don't even shoot a gun, don't know how to." Somebody else at the table was shaking his head. He thought I was a nut. Nobody would have thought anybody would take a potshot at the President, this was America.

What really troubled me was that a lot of people in the South didn't like Kennedy being the President. He had done the school integrations and he was a hated man in some places. Knowing that Southerners were in the audience and that some of them might bear a grudge, that crossed my mind. He had had so many problems with the Southerners. Someone could have taken out the whole cabinet and where would we have been?

I knew about security because there had been a lot of killing of European leaders during the war. But on this night in 1963, I had a very good view of President Kennedy and I know I could have shot him from where I sat. Horrible isn't it?

I still have the actual invitation to the dinner, visitors' passes, program, guest list, and pictures. I'm probably one of the few people who picked these souvenirs up and brought them home. These bronze medallions were souvenirs on the table for each guest, along with the programs which bore our names. They were meant to be taken by the guests. Most people didn't take them when they left but I took mine. I wish I had taken some of the others. I only came home with two medallions and two programs. I could have had 500 of these, no doubt. What a pity. I bet a lot of people were kicking themselves later.

Four-inch bronze medallions were keepsakes given to those who attended the B'nai Brith Anti-Defamation League's 50th anniversary dinner in Washington, D.C. Jasmine has preserved them for more than 50 years.

Melvin said, "Why are you taking these home? We have no room in the luggage."

I answered, "Someday they'll be valuable to our family, Melvin." Instinct told me to walk about the tables and pick them up, but I thought that looked terrible. So I just took the gift items from my table.

When I got home, I just kept talking about the lack of security. I can't believe that for a presidential dinner, with strangers from everywhere, we'd been fingerprinted before we went, but nobody stopped me on the away into the dinner.

A few months later, when Kennedy was assassinated, I told Melvin, "See what I told you?" A person off the street could have knocked me out in the restroom and taken my place.

Melvin said, "You see shadows around every corner." That's why I kept so much of my thoughts quiet. People may think I'm crazy, but I didn't just say it after the fact; the security was terrible.

When the President was shot that November, the girls were in school. I had flown to Canada for my younger sister's wedding. I stayed with my mother for a week. We had a babysitter at home for the children and Melvin was going to meet me in Chicago for his cousin's wedding. I went to a hairdresser two days before Kennedy was shot. I didn't want to look like a shaggy dog. And the woman said, "Isn't that terrible about what happened to the mayor of Toronto?" He was only 43 years old and dropped dead on the golf course. He had a severe heart condition that apparently no one knew about. Everybody was in shock from that.

Turn around two days later, I was back in the beauty shop and the beautician said, "Did you hear about the President?"

"What president?" I asked.

"The President of the United States. He's been shot."

I said, "Are you serious?" Unfortunately, she was. Melvin heard about it on the plane flying to Chicago to meet me. It was a shock to everybody. The awful thing was that I'd seen in Washington that there was something terribly wrong with his security. I can never forgive myself for not speaking up to someone about it.

PART III: WIFE, MOTHER, PHILANTHROPIST

Chapter 24

My life during this time was busy. In addition to the organizations and committees, I continued performing whenever I got a chance.

While the children were at home, and after they had left the nest, I did semi-professional acting at the Lyric Theater, the Jewel Box, and the Theater in the Round, all in Oklahoma City, and Shawnee Little Theater. At the Shawnee theater, the performers are never paid. I loved working there for that reason.

Jasmine played in *My Fair Lady* in both the Lyric Theater and the Shawnee Little Theater. Jasmine loved her return to the theater as a semi-professional.

My first production in Oklahoma was *Music Man*, in which I played the pianola girl, Ethel Tofflemeyer. I did *My Fair Lady* and *Oliver* at both the Lyric and in Shawnee. I was in *A Day in the Death of Joe Egg* at the Theater in the Round, and *See How They Run* at the Jewel Box. And in Seminole, I was in the Arts Council's *Black Coffee*, an Agatha Christie mystery. I've enjoyed performing in each one.

Jasmine, center, played Mrs. Higgins in Shawnee Little Theater's production of *My Fair Lady* in January and February, 1995. She was joined by Kay Shields, Chris Wagner, Julie Hagler, Bill McDonald, David Byland, and Jo Lewis.

I met former Attorney General and president of Oklahoma City University Robert Henry at Shawnee Little Theater and we became fast friends. I played his

Jasmine played Mrs. Bedwin, the housekeeper in the Lyric Theater's production of *Oliver*. She sang "Where Is Love" to Oliver.

mother-in-law Lady Alice, the wife of Sir Thomas More, in *A Man for All Seasons*. Every time I saw him after that, he'd say, "Oh, there's my mother-in-law" and grin. I met very nice people in the shows.

There were a bunch of us often working together. A lot of those who worked so hard in small parts in these shows are getting older now and no longer performing. Most of us really liked each other. We'd see each other at auditions and say, "Not you again," but it was a lot of fun.

When I was performing in *Music Man* at the Lyric Theater,

we were rehearsing from 10 in the morning to 10 at night. I was both dancing and singing. The cast included Jean Amick and her husband Judge John Amick, who was a professor at Oklahoma City University. One day Jean said, "It's raining cats and dogs outside. You're not going home, you're staying with me. Give me your phone number; I'm calling Melvin."

He said he was absolutely worried and praying I wouldn't come home. We didn't have cell phones then. I said, "Jean wants me to stay with her." She put me up another time, too. We became good friends.

Their son, Alan, was also in the cast. Alan was about 10 at the time. About two years later, we were no longer working together, but I used to hear from her every once in awhile. She was a piano teacher and kept busy. One day she called and said, "I have a very large favor to ask of you."

"Ask away," I said. "You've done favors for me. I've stayed with you and you never let me pay for anything."

She said, "You know we sat up talking half the night. I enjoyed your company. That was payment enough."

Alan had a chance to audition in New York for *The King and I* as Anna's English son. He needed a British accent. I said I'd be glad to help, but I couldn't come up there all the time. My kids were very involved in school activities and I was forever having to drive them somewhere, usually out of town.

"Come here and bring Alan with you, and we'll talk and he can hear how I pronounce words," I said. I told her to bring him and his script and I would read it into a tape recorder as I would say it. I would say each word slowly and clearly so he could hear. We worked for about three weeks, him coming to Seminole two or three times a week and I went up to Oklahoma City a couple of times. For weeks, his mother said he studied so hard he barely came out of his room. He was determined to get the role.

He went to the audition and there were tons of kids, including four boys from Canada, who had very good accents. And he won. I said, "You've done me proud." After the audition, he had been asked where he got his English accent, because he was from Oklahoma. He told them he had an English friend.

The King and I opened in 1977. I couldn't go to opening night, but we were lucky enough to go see it three or four nights after opening. Yul Brynner was playing in it. When Alan introduced me to the cast, he said, "This is my diction teacher." The critics even commented on his English accent.

Alan was so good, I thought he would stay in show business. He was offered several jobs and there were several who wanted to manage him. When you get a manager, you're on the way.

Alan stayed with the show about a year, but he was growing so fast, and it was time for him to leave. He'd had all kinds of offers; he was a really sweet and talented kid. Later Jean wrote to me that Alan loved show business and was

During the 1967 Miss Seminole Pageant, Jasmine, above left, played Phyllis Diller, to the enjoyment of Miss America Jane Jayroe. The Morans produced the pageant for seven years.

having a wonderful time, but he missed living in Oklahoma.

Jean said he came home to think about it. He decided to go into aviation. He is a pilot now, I think for Virgin America Airlines, and loves his job.

During these very creative years, I was on *The Ida B Show* on Channel 4 in Oklahoma City three times, where I sang and talked about Scottish dancing. I was also in a couple of programs on Ada's Channel 10.

Melvin and I produced the Miss Seminole Pageant for

During the Morans' tenure coordinating the Miss Seminole Pageant, Jasmine frequently enjoyed playing comic characters. She sang "Feudin', Fussin' and a Fightin'" from *Annie Get Your Gun* with Bill Hyden.

Jasmine and Karen White sing "We're a Couple of Swells" during a Miss Seminole Pageant. The song is from the musical film *Easter Parade* starring Judy Garland and Fred Astaire.

seven years. It was in the Miss America circuit, and I also trained the girls on how to walk and what to say when speaking to the judges. Mel and I were judges in other Oklahoma pageants five or six times and enjoyed that period of time.

I performed with the Selectones, a singing group organized in Seminole in May 1967 by Corinna Powell, a local singer. Membership ranged from 24 to 30 singers. We practiced each Monday night and

Isla Mae and Junior Phillips were the Morans' best friends for many years and accompanied them on many trips and outings. Isla Mae Phillips also accompanied the Selectones, a singing group from Seminole.

sang at area civic club dinners and meetings, churches, and social events.

Isla Mae Phillips accompanied us on piano. For many years, she and her husband Junior were Melvin's and my best friends. Isla Mae was my accompanist when I occasionally sang at other civic events and at auditions. She did a terrific job.

The Selectones' concerts were held in Seminole, Oklahoma City, Maud, Shawnee, Wewoka, Holdenville, and McAlester. We performed on the Hudson Brothers' TV show, *The Ida B Show,* and on Channel 13. We also performed in a Christmas concert at Seminole High School.

The Selectones didn't perform only for the joy of performing. During our six years together, we awarded scholarships, and contributed to the music fund at Seminole Junior College, and to a band uniform fund at Seminole High School.

Corinna directed the group until 1972, when she moved to Hollis. It was then directed by Isla Mae and, later, by Jerry Lynn, who had served as our pianist and were both integral parts of the Selectones. The Selectones disbanded in 1973.

We met again 22 years later, in 1995, for a reunion at Adriano's Restaurant in Seminole. Besides me, others attending the reunion were Jerry Lynn, Jerry Sullivan, Lena Mae Smith, Linda Parkhurst, Verna Gallemore, Esther Snell, Allene Grounds, Barbara Mendenhall, Norma Wilcox, Wynema Melton, Billye Coates, Thelma Lilly, Elaine Allison, and Vivian Morris.

PART III: WIFE, MOTHER, PHILANTHROPIST

Chapter 25

In the mid 1970s, there was an historic event in Seminole that was nearly catastrophic for our small town, and would have been if a few people had not acted as they did.

We lived on Phelps Drive. When I drove in to Safeway, I noticed many vehicles with South Dakota license plates. Several had the Native American symbol in the window, the arm raised holding a tommy gun, like a small machine gun. I assumed there was a pow wow. When I left, I noticed a lot of the cars in the parking lot had a pamphlet under the wipers with the symbol of the American Indian Movement (AIM).

I was barely home when my neighbor, Tommy Jones, called. Her husband, Les, owned Jones Jewelry Store on Main Street. Melvin was mayor at the time. Tommy said there was something I needed to know. She was of Native American heritage and she said one of Russell Means' groups was in town and was going to start trouble. Means did not come himself, but had called a meeting of all the Indian tribes and told them they needed to fight to get Seminole back. I said, "You're kidding." Mel, as mayor, was in the heart of it. It scared me to death.

Russell Means [1939-2012] was the first national director of the American Indian Movement [AIM]. He helped organize notable events that attracted national and international media coverage on issues of Native peoples. He participated in the 1969 Alcatraz occupation and the 1972 armed stand-off between more than 300 Lakota and AIM activists against the FBI at Wounded Knee, which lasted for 71 days. It was AIM's best-known action. Means was also an actor and can be seen in *Last of the Mohicans* and *Natural Born Killers*. - biography.com

Tommy said protesters had taken over a building downtown on Oak Street and put a poster in the window. It was almost across from Helen Adams' Lunch 'n' Such back door. Tommy always parked out there when she came down to help out at the jewelry store. She nearly had a fit when she saw what was happening. The AIM movement had moved into the store across Oak Street and was setting up house, meaning they were planning on staying and causing trouble.

Bill Wantland, who was a tribal litigator and city judge at the time, got a whiff of it. Bill and Melvin met with them. The protestors had a pamphlet that said something like, "I hereby give Seminole back to the Indians." They threw it down on the desk and said, "Sign this." Melvin said, "Who are you?" He said, "I won't sign anything without reading it."

He convinced them to leave it with him so he could look it over. But he pointed out that the mayor doesn't own Seminole, so therefore could not give it back. They were incensed; they wanted notoriety. They wanted the town to be held hostage. They scheduled to meet at 4:00 p.m. and they called all the TV channels. One or two TV stations sent reporters. Melvin told them nothing was going on and scheduled to meet the protestors the next day instead.

I was down at Adwan's, a dress shop. I'd had a dress altered.

Two men came in the door. One held up a badge and then locked the door and pulled down the blinds. They pushed us away from the windows. I got pushed and almost fell down. My knees were already knocking.

"We understand there's going to be trouble," they said. The AIM protesters were planning a parade and these men from the FBI were trying to circumvent it. Four open cars loaded with AIM protestors, some with guns, came by. At the end of their parade route, they were arrested and taken away. The FBI agents in Adwan's raised the blinds and unlocked the doors and left. I'd had some small clue about what was going on, but the others in the store had none.

That night someone tried to set fire to the railroad bridge that crosses over State Highway 9 near Earlsboro, but it was mostly concrete and wouldn't ignite. They ran away, but someone saw them. The protestors wanted to isolate Seminole. Tommy said the locals wouldn't join with them. We knew their ancestors had been treated badly, but there was nothing we could do about it now. The townspeople and the Native Americans all lived peaceably together here and everyone was happy.

The AIM people were here for five days, maybe a week. They wanted to make an example of Seminole. If we'd given them the publicity they wanted, it could have been a second Wounded Knee, but they were unable to stir up any sympathy from the local Native Americans. Bill and Melvin managed to keep the lid on the story. Only about 10 people ever knew what really nearly happened.

PART III: WIFE, MOTHER, PHILANTHROPIST

Chapter 26

One refrain that has repeated my whole life has been a love of animals. My mother was a very compassionate person. She always looked tough, but she was Jell-O inside. She rescued animals, too. I'd bring them home and she would say, "We can't afford to keep it. Oh, look at those eyes." Animals are trustworthy, they love you. When they give you love, they really give all their love—even if some of us are not worthy of their trust.

I think I have been an animal rights activist since I was a child, but it's not just about animals. I have a respect for all living things.

I've seen a lot over the years; life has taken so many turns. Is there a connection between the death I saw as a small child during the war and my abhorrence to violence as an adult? There has to be.

As a child, I remember going home for the weekend with a friend from a well-to-do family. We were coming from the train station.

In the summer of 1994, Jasmine and her cat Tip share a sofa for a nap. Pets have been a constant in Jasmine's life since she moved to the U.S.A.

In England they had all these roads with hedges alongside that go this way and that. The shortest way was about a mile. They had a beautiful home in Surrey. It was the first time I'd been there.

We could hear the awful screams walking to her home, carrying our books. Then we heard growling and snarling, and came around a hedge. All the horsemen were sitting on horses watching the dogs tearing the fox to pieces, tearing him to shreds. My friend started beating on the man who had cut off the tail, it was still dripping blood. I was screaming. It was such a disturbing scene. Is this sport? It was the most awful thing. I'll remember to my dying day that animal screaming.

When we got to her home, we were still crying, weeping. We told her mother that we had just come upon a foxhunt. She said, "Let's talk about it." She said there are things we don't like, that we can't do anything about. It was a terrible thing. We were sick with horror.

From then on, whether it is a child or an animal, I decided that I will do whatever I can, even if I lost my life trying. I can't sit and say nothing or do nothing. I guess that's when I became an animal rights activist. I had seen things before that disturbed me, but I never saw anything like that. The fox was screaming, terrible, piercing screams. I could never get that scream out of my mind. How could they just sit there and allow the animal to be torn to pieces? If they had to kill it, kill it. Why sit there and watch it be tortured?

We've seen moose and bear in the wild, things that God created. He put them in nature. I see people who want to destroy them. The white seals, they beat them to death for their fur. The horror is disgusting to me.

Some of my biggest joys have been seeing tranquil fields of cattle. There are several places on the way to Shawnee where they used to keep a lot of cattle; there's not so many now. I know we eat them and I know their lives are not the happiest. We barbarically kill cows. I know the way they're taken out of the world. But to think they had at least some joy before they died is a pleasure to me.

There was a Humane Society in Seminole when I first came in the 1950s, but it was just three people with no rules or regulations. Nobody could actually do anything when we saw animals that were abused. There were all these cats running around downtown, looking for food in garbage cans. There wasn't anybody to take care of them; oh, someone would put down a bowl of milk occasionally. I was so disgusted. It wasn't a good image for Seminole. I found some people of the same ilk as myself—Teresa Smith, LaVere Bishop, and Tandi Coates are some that I can think of at the moment— and we started to get ideas on what we might do. So the Humane Society has mushroomed over the years.

As head of the Humane Society, I've sometimes had to get tough with people. I say, "I'm going to come back and visit you and if I don't see improvement, we're going to bring the sheriff and impound these animals."

Melvin said, "You lied."

"Yes, but I'm going to take care of it," I replied.

Jasmine and her cat Spats, rescued from the Seminole animal shelter, sit at the kitchen table during interviews for this book. Spats came and went at will, always showing up in time for dinner.

One man called me a "bitch." I told him everyone calls me that.

We passed a dog tied too closely to his doghouse with no food or water. I stopped and tried to explain it to the landowner. He told me to get off his property. I know they just think I'm a do-gooder. But I passed by again in a couple of days and the dog was on higher ground with a longer leash. He had two bowls of dry food.

People call and tell me when they see animals being neglected or abused. Many could handle the problems themselves. It's their next door neighbor, or something they've seen in the field. Instead of saying, "Don't you think you should be taking care of this?" I just say, "Give me the address." The sheriff's department is usually pretty good. The police will come sometimes, but I can get put out with them. They say I can get ferocious. I realize you have to be civilized in these situations, but I don't always feel like I have the time to waste. My final statement is that I have to try to make these people feel guilty, to make them realize what they are doing is wrong. God did not put us on Earth to destroy everything.

It's taken a long time for the Humane Society to reach the goals we planned for many years. With many wonderful people helping physically and financially, I was able to fund the new shelter. Now we finally have a building to house unwanted, abused, and sick animals. And we try to find them good homes for the rest of their lives. The time and effort spent over the years to try to get the shelter built has been worth all the trouble, especially now seeing the shelter being taken care of by young people. They do their jobs with love and respect for the animals and I am so proud of what I see today. I hope it continues for many generations to expand and grow and make people aware that the animals we live with are God's gift to us just as our children are. The animals are children in fur coats and need our love and help too.

Jasmine's love for animals is legendary. She gives loving attention to her pets Spats and Roxie.

I have often wondered why God chose to fill the ark with animals instead of more human beings. I believe it was because He wanted us to learn to love and respect animals. Even though, as meat eaters, we do take their lives. We still need to know and respect the animals during their lifetimes and not torture them. I believe that is what God had in mind.

PART III: WIFE, MOTHER, PHILANTHROPIST

Chapter 27

One of the most rewarding projects of my life has certainly been the Jasmine Moran Children's Museum. It all started in August of 1988 when we were taking our daughter Marilyn, her husband Bill, and our two granddaughters for a holiday on Mackinac Island in northern Michigan. We had a couple of days before our reservation and decided to find something the children would enjoy. We were looking at brochures about Flint, Michigan, and decided to go have a look at the museum there.

It was very small, in the middle of a lot of buildings, with no parking. People parked on the street with the workers in the other buildings. We had no idea what to expect. We went in and were intrigued. There were lots of old things: typewriters, curling irons, telephones, old toasters. Not antiques, just old sewing machines and bicycles you could take apart and put back together. The idea was to use your imagination, stimulate your own brain waves. And it worked. A lot of people were playing with them. I played with a sewing machine like my mother had.

We were so excited about what we saw that we sent Melvin back to the hotel to get our video camera. We decided we'd like to have a children's museum in our town, but we thought that we could work on something more. I liked the idea of creating a play place, but we liked the idea of using something besides old toasters. We started with baby steps that turned into gigantic steps.

Nobody believed a world-class children's museum could survive in a small town of 7,500, an hour from the closest big city. Who would come? Who would volunteer and support it?

I thought it would be a joy to the local children. Melvin and I were both concerned about the latchkey children, stuck in front of the television while their parents were both working. We wanted to stimulate them. Moms and dads are tired after work and don't have much time or strength to stimulate the kids. So most

Melvin and Jasmine show off a mural wall in the Jasmine Moran Children's Museum. Their signature project opened in 1993.

The inside of the Jasmine Moran Children's Museum is divided into small "storefronts," marking areas where children get to play at being grown-ups. In the "Handi-Capable" exhibit, children learn what it's like to live with physical limitations.

of those kids just did their homework and went to bed.

But we wanted to reach more than just the children in Seminole. We decided that if ours was to be a success, it had to be extra special to attract families from long distances; we decided to make it the best one in the country.

We were babes in the woods. We knew this town needed something. It was during the oil bust of the 1980s and Seminole was beginning to look like a ghost town. We didn't want to see that happen. We hoped the museum could bring tourism to our small town.

We thought, if we're not going to do this, there is no point in having wealth. We've had wealthy friends who did wonderful things with their money and they were quiet with it. I always wondered why people have private jets and their own hotel rooms; we always travel coach. If you don't do good with money, then I don't know why God gave it to you.

I tell Melvin that he made a lot of money taking something from the ground and that if you put nothing back, you have raped the earth. You can only wear so many shoes, so many pairs of pants. A life like that would drive me nuts. I didn't come from it and I wouldn't want it. Besides that, my mother would stand up in her grave and say, "If you can't do better than that, you should just leave."

So Melvin planned his infamous lunch in October 1988—15 educators and mothers at the Gusher Inn. After showing his video from Flint, Michigan, everybody signed on, although almost everyone told us later that they couldn't believe the idea would work. Marci Donaho was there, almost by accident, and her signing on turned out to be divine providence. Melvin and I believe she is a major reason for the museum's success. She has been the director since Tommy Mills left and continues to inspire us with ideas and enthusiasm every day. Melvin and I often say Marci should be named co-founder, along with

Jasmine and the Jasmine Moran Children's Museum Director Marci Donaho have enjoyed a close relationship. Here they are pictured after a board meeting in front of the museum's train mural.

us. Her fingerprints are on every inch of the museum.

We got a board together and started passing around ideas, and the museum came from there. Melvin did much of the fundraising early on, asking for grants and donations from foundations, corporations, and individuals, and I helped when I could. We know a lot of people professionally and socially and many doors opened for us. Later, after Marci became director, she also became the principal fundraiser. People like Gene Rainbolt, Robert Henry, David Boren, Ann Alspaugh, and many others, without them and their support and introductions, there would likely be no museum today.

Yes, we are proud of what has been accomplished. Amazed, really. If we had realized how much the museum would grow and the number of people coming from all over the world to visit, we wouldn't have believed it possible.

Our beginnings were very humble. The Power Transmission building, when we bought it, wasn't very accessible. But it came with eleven acres of land, and we've been able to buy much of the surrounding property as well. Everybody was very nice to help renovate the facility, many volunteering their time and donating their money.

At first, we planned to call it The Moran Family Children's Museum, but Melvin thought that was too wordy. After a trip to

Colorado, where I became very ill, he changed the name to the Jasmine Moran Children's Museum without telling me. I would have said, "No thanks." There are two reasons to name something after someone. If they're dead, it's okay, but if you do it while they're still alive, to me it feels like showing off. The way I was brought up, you don't shout it out if you do good things, you be quiet about it. My mother did so many things to help people and Melvin's mother was the same way—she always sat in the back of the bus with the African Americans. It was her way of showing that she wasn't better than they were. But Melvin didn't consult me about the name change and it was too late.

The average time it takes to open a museum is five years. Ours opened on January 23, 1993, four years and three months after our initial lunch. Now, at almost 25 years old, it has expanded to 42,000 square feet inside and 12 acres outside. We celebrated our 1-millionth visitor several years ago. We are proud to have been recognized with many awards and accolades.

The Flint Children's Museum had 20,000 annual visitors. So that number became our goal. We had not considered the fact that the population of Flint is 20 times the population of Seminole. But in 2016 our visitors numbered 72,000.

The museum's front was renovated in 2012 to make room for a new dinosaur exhibit. The new front was designed and painted by Seminole area artist April Ledbetter Jones.

PART III: WIFE, MOTHER, PHILANTHROPIST

Chapter 28

My later years have been fraught with illness and injury, but I try never to let it get me down. I call myself an accident waiting to happen...and it usually does. Every time I go to a new doctor, they say, "You have so many problems." But I am not alone. Many people do.

The first serious injury was a torn patella, a knee injury that happened while rehearsing for *Oliver* at Shawnee Little Theater. I was playing the housekeeper. When I came out of the bright lights of the green room into the darkness of the parking lot, someone had moved a concrete block that had been used to hold open the back door.

My toe hit the block and I realized what it was, but I had my music with me, my purse, book, keys, and suddenly I was stumbling forward. I knew I was going to hit something going down, so I thought I'd better throw myself backwards, I have a nice big bottom, it won't be so bad to hit that, I thought. So I did.

Two of the chorus girls had already gone to their cars. As I walked out of the door, they turned on headlights and they said they saw me do a double somersault and came down with my knee on the concrete block. I didn't know I could even do one somersault, much less two.

They dragged me back into the green room and my knee was already enormous. I couldn't stand on my foot. The stage director and her husband took me to the emergency room. The female intern told me nothing was broken, but I'd have to stay off my feet for five days. But the play opened in five days. She gave me something for pain.

I packed the leg in ice, but didn't sleep much that night. I stayed off my foot as much as possible at first, and then tried to return to rehearsal. Mel drove me to Shawnee and waited for me to finish rehearsals. But walking through my part was very painful and slow. The play was opening so we didn't have any more time for me to take off. I didn't have an understudy, so I had to go on. I continued to rehearse as best as I could until the day before opening.

At the dress rehearsal, I could still hardly walk. I was supposed to wear high-heeled shoes and climb the stairs, which was not easy. I had to climb to little Oliver's bedroom in front of the audience and sing to him. He sings to me, "Where is love?" and I sing back to him. The show was open seven days and I did the whole seven days. I had to keep my knee bound up the whole time and I was in terrible, terrible pain, but we got through the show.

I finally decided I needed to go to an orthopedic specialist, a very fine doctor at McBride, Dr. Stephen Tkach, who had been recommended to me. By the time I got an appointment, it had been a good two weeks since the accident. He said, "Why

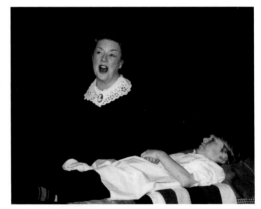

Jasmine was rehearsing for *Oliver* at Shawnee Little Theater when she fell and tore her patella. She continued to rehearse and perform, wearing high heels and climbing stairs, until the production ended about two weeks later.

didn't you come here after the emergency room? You must have been in terrible pain. I don't even know how you got into this office. Your patella is ripped off."

He said that, if I could stand pain like this, I should just walk on it as long as I could and come back when I couldn't stand the pain any longer. He said, "The surgery I'm going to have to put you through is really bad and you'll be lucky to get 10 years on the replacement knee. If you can tolerate this much pain, I suggest you just keep going and hopefully we will only have to replace it one time."

So I continued walking on it for about three years. Then my daughter Marilyn and I had a three-day weekend planned in Chicago. We had a wonderful time, went to a comedy club and a wonderful art museum. We walked and my knee hurt, but it wasn't agony. We'd had a lovely dinner at an Italian restaurant and we were walking to our hotel about five blocks away when my knee locked behind me. I couldn't bring it forward and I nearly fell.

I couldn't walk and Marilyn asked how we were going to get back to the hotel. I said we would have to go slowly and I'd have to drag it. She suggested a cab and I said, "How will I get in?" She suggested maybe hang it out the window.

And that's what we did. I got in on the passenger side, rolled the window, and hung it out the window. When we got to the hotel, we had to wait until everybody got off the elevator so I could go in sideways with my leg dragging behind me. She ran me a bath. She thought maybe it would relax me. I said I hoped so. We had to struggle like the devil to get me into it. I thought she was going to kill me and she thought the same because I wouldn't let go of her. I was flying home the next day and knew I'd need to see the doctor as soon as I got home. But she said, "How are you going to get on the airplane?"

At the airport, we told them at the desk about what had

happened. We asked if I could have two seats, but they said no, they were fully booked. I said, "I can't hang my leg out in the aisle, people are coming up and down." Finally they said I could go into first class, where they found two seats. I sat in the window seat on the left side of the plane on my left hip with my right leg hanging out into the aisle.

It was terrible getting on the plane. The pilot, stewardess, and a passenger helped me to climb up the stairs to the plane. They all had their hands around me and when they would say jump, the pilot would pull me forward to the next step. There were probably 10 steps. It was awful, but we made it.

I didn't tell Melvin what had happened, so when I got in to Oklahoma City, he saw me and said, "What has happened to you?"

"You wouldn't believe me," I said.

"Yes, I would. You flew home like that?"

"Yes, everyone had to wobble around my leg while it hung in the plane's aisle. It didn't hurt, but it was a real nuisance."

Dr. Tkach did the surgery as soon as possible because he was leaving on holiday the next day. The surgery was painful, but went well. Rehab was hell on earth. I had never been in more pain in my life. The therapist kept trying to get me to stretch my leg over a ball. He would say, "You're just not trying. Don't be lazy."

"You're not in my skin, you don't know," I'd exclaim.

"If you aren't going to try, you're never going to walk again."

I said, "I'm a dancer, I've danced all my life. I know what pain is. If you saw how bad my feet are, you'd know." I was angry at his reluctance to help me further my goals, but he seemed to just be slapping me in the face and that was not helping.

I finally told him he was dismissed. In my wheelchair, I went back to my room and cried for about 30 minutes. How dare he say things like that to me? What a terrible thing to say to someone who had just undergone the surgery I had! And expecting me to do impossible things three days after surgery! I thought, "I'll be damned if I'm going to spend my life in a wheelchair. I'm going to walk if it's the last thing I do."

I went back down to the therapy room and there was another therapist who seemed to be very patient. I approached her and said, "I'd like you to be my therapist; do you have any spare time?" She said "no."

"I'll take whatever you have," I said. She asked what happened to my therapist.

"He told me I'd never walk again," I told her.

"That was a terrible thing to tell someone," she said.

"Yesterday was my first day here. I'm really not putting on, I really can't put my leg over a ball," I said.

"Well, I won't pressure you, but we'll do everything we can to get you on your feet."

"Believe me, I want to be on my feet," I told her.

She asked if I would skip breakfast and work with her; she got in at 7:00 a.m. and we could work until 9:00 a.m. We even worked through her lunch; she brought sandwiches and shared them with me. She worked the tail off me. I sweated like a pig. The hospital had a machine that attaches to your leg. It helps you move your leg back and forth and I could take it to my room to use it. I worked on that from 2:00 p.m. until 9:00 p.m. for a number of days. I had supper in bed. I worked from seven to eight hours a day on the machine, every single day, when my time was not taken up with therapy. I worked with the therapist every lunchtime and every breakfast until I got my knee back in shape. I was walking with a cane in eight days; though it was very painful, I was able to stand on it.

One day I passed the first therapist. "Never walk again, huh?" I said. "Much you know." I should have beaten him with my cane. I was still so aggravated at him.

When the doctor came back from his trip, he saw me with the cane and he said, "Good Lord, Jasmine, you're walking much better than I expected after what I had to do to you. I didn't expect you to be walking like this for another two months."

I said, "Are you serious?"

"Yes, I'm serious. You're one big metal mess of nails and bolts."

I said, "Wait a minute, what did you have to do to me?"

He had come to the hospital the morning he left for vacation and he told Melvin while I was unconscious, that he had to do a tremendous amount of work on my knee, much more than he had anticipated, as I had damaged tendons, nerves, and ligaments. Therefore he expected to see me upon his return still on crutches or in a wheelchair. When I walked in with a cane, he was astonished. Melvin never told me any of this. I assume Melvin thought I had heard all this from the doctor, but I did not know how serious the surgery was.

Not long after my knee surgery, I awoke one morning feeling very tired. This was while we lived at 2300 Morningside Drive. Mel normally leaves about 8:30 a.m. but he was in the kitchen and he said something to me. I said, "I had a very bad night. I couldn't sleep and I have an awful headache. My head is buzzing." He looked at me and didn't say anything. I said, "I have a terrible headache. I'm not feeling very well." He said something to me and I didn't understand a word he said. I said, "That's not funny. I have a nasty headache. Why make garbage talk?" It sounded like people talking in tongues. He said something else and I burst into tears. I finally realized he couldn't understand what I was saying and I didn't understand what he was saying. So I went to the pad near the phone and wrote the word "stroke" with a question mark. When I looked at it, it was all over the paper. I thought I had written neatly.

He went straight to the phone and called the doctor, and said, "I think Jasmine might have had a stroke."

We went to the doctor, who referred me to a neurologist. He said, "You are very lucky. Bleeding in the brain caused the stroke, but there isn't a lot of damage and it's in an area where you don't have a lot of activity." He said it might leave me a little paralyzed and with either short- or long-term memory loss.

I was left slightly paralyzed in my right hand, but I was still able to write, though it was hard to grasp a pen. During that period of time, I recognized faces, but didn't remember names. People would say, "Hello, Jasmine," in the grocery store, but I couldn't tell you who they were. Melvin made a tape for the phone, explaining it to people who called. It was a good six weeks before I could understand people again.

When I had my knee surgery done, I already had my little red car. I won't give up my little red car. It's a Buick, and I've had it since 1990. It doesn't have many miles on it and I have put on every one of those miles myself. I'm "the little old lady from Pasadena." I've been to California in it once, and to Canada several times to see my family. I've driven it to Wisconsin to see my kids at summer camp. But it's primarily driven around Seminole, Shawnee, Wewoka, and Oklahoma City on occasion. I can go anywhere. It parks easily and I don't have to look between the steering wheel and the dash because I can see over it. Actually I could lay three people down in the trunk. It's enormous. When I go grocery shopping, I like to have lots of room. It's a convenient car with marvelous trunk space and it is all steel, no plastic anywhere. The interior is well made with some leather parts. It has all the new innovations of the 1990s. It's very maneuverable.

Melvin says I need a new car. I say, "It goes when I want it to go, mind your own business, I'm not giving up that car." It's still going, there is nothing major wrong with it. I tell him, "If you want to buy a new car, buy one for yourself. Mine goes through all kinds of bumps and it's still running. I shall be driving that car until the day I die."

I recently ran through the back of the garage. I had a problem with the type of shoe I was wearing. It slid under the accelerator while I was trying to park the car. The car sustained pretty heavy damage in the front end, but no motor injuries.

The insurance company refused to pay me to get it fixed. They said it would cost too much considering how old it is. I held out because my car is made of steel and I did not want a plastic car. I fought like a dog to keep my car. The insurance company gave me about half what it cost to fix it. They wanted to junk it. But they finally did some checking around and found that this is now considered a classic car. Everything on it is hard to replace, but still possible. We found pieces to replace the front end and I am now driving it again. Mel said I was very lucky to be in that car when I went through the garage instead of his car, a two-year-old Buick. I was totally unhurt, not even a scratch. His car has already had a number of dents removed from it, where car doors hit it. My description of his car: fancy looking and made of tissue paper. He gets mad when I call it tissue paper. I'll keep mine any day.

Before I got that car, I had a Pontiac. I was involved in a hit-and-run car accident in the 1980s, which further compromised my health. I was turning left and a man ran the stop sign and hit my car full blast on the passenger side in front of the funeral home on Milt Phillips and Strother in Seminole. The impact knocked me out and I fell across the front seat. The windshield broke and glass fell all over me. When I came to, there was a man at the window, saying, "Thank God! I thought you had broken your neck." He was a stunt man at Frontier City and had been on the phone at the convenience store across the street. He had seen cowboys take falls and said that the hit I took could have broken my neck.

I went to the hospital, but my worst pain at the time was a toenail that was nearly ripped off from where my sandal had gone under the accelerator. The next day I started having a headache, dreadful pain like an electric shock from my neck into my head. For two years we went to doctors, but never really realized it was because of the accident. I was in physical therapy for two years and in constant pain, despite any pain medication.

The doctors all tell me my vertebrae are like mush, part because of the accident and part is because of age. Part of the problem is that the vertebrae just disintegrated, and the rest is just wear and tear. My doctor told me I have to wear a brace in the car, because if the car was hit from the side, it could break my neck or what little I have left. I have to be very cautious. When I sit in a movie theater or where my neck must be held rigid, on planes or for any form of travel, I have to wear my neck brace.

I had constant headaches, fingers of pain running up the back of my head, all the time. For two years, I was never without pain. And I can't take pain killers: codeine makes me pass out and Tylenol affects my stomach. I was miserable until I met Lynn Wieck, who is a massage therapist.

After the first day with Lynn working on my neck and shoulders, I came home, and I was not hurting. I wasn't hurting that night and the pain was minimal for the next two days. I decided it was a miracle and have been going to her for eight or 10 years now. She keeps my neck and shoulders in relatively good shape and without pain.

IN RETROSPECT

Chapter 29

It's been a long time since I went back to Hornchurch.
Maybe 45 years? It had grown a little, but it was still a small town.
I recognized the general layout. Hornchurch's main "claim to fame"
was the old 14th century houses near Main Street; to have something
that old and still in that good shape was wonderful, a real tourist
attraction. They were still being lived in up until the war. After that
the government maintained them. But when I went back, they had
been torn down and replaced with white-washed concrete apartments,
awful, modernistic looking apartment buildings. I was so shocked
when I saw that, I burst into tears.

A little man walking by with a cane saw the tears running
down my cheeks and said, "I feel the same way. The stupid council said
they were too expensive to maintain."

Our little bungalow and the council houses where we lived
were all still there, nothing glamorous, not the kind of house you
take someone all the way to England to see. I remember thinking
the bungalow was a magnificent palace. There were a lot of memories
there.

Not long after I had moved to the U.S. from Europe, I visited

Dunkirk and Normandy, where the D-Day landing in June, 1944, marked the turning point of the war. More than 425,000 soldiers are believed to have died at Normandy. I imagined a sea of dead bodies lying on the beach.

Normandy is a small town, and there is such a feeling of reverence there. The cemetery feels like you are visiting an open air church. All those hundreds of graves of young people, mostly under the age of 30, made me realize how grateful we should be for their determination and courage. You can feel their spirit there. I am so proud that there are people who would give up their lives to better the lives of others. We should realize how lucky we are that there are people who have done that for us and continue to honor them.

I spent the whole time there blowing my nose and mopping my eyes. We were with a tour, but we stayed behind about five days to talk to people there. We sat in restaurants. We saw how grateful the people were to both our countries, Britain and the U.S., by how respectful they were to those who visited. Even people who hadn't even been born during the war were so respectful. They know they would not have been free but for those who gave their lives. People didn't want us to pay for our own food, always wanting to buy us a beer. They were so respectful I was boggled. The shadow of death hung over those beaches. It was poignant and sad. The death toll was awful: French, Poles, English, Scottish, Irish, Australians, Canadians. Touring these places you felt like you had lost a relative there yourself.

And what do we Americans do on the day that is supposed to be reserved to honor these people? We watch ballgames or go to the lake instead of reflecting. We should use the day for introspection, for being thankful that you can still be here, unlike all those who are gone from their families. I still feel this way. We don't honor the dead like we should.

We were also moved by the price paid for freedom during the 66th anniversary dedication to the USS *Oklahoma* memorial at Pearl Harbor. I was especially interested because of my World War II past, and my subsequent life in Oklahoma.

> On Dec. 7, 2007, to commemorate the 66th anniversary of the bombing at Pearl Harbor, a memorial was dedicated to the USS *Oklahoma*, one of the four ships sunk by the Japanese. A total of more than 2,400 Americans died, including 429 who had been aboard the USS *Oklahoma*. The ship was towed across the harbor in 1943 and was decommissioned on Sept. 1, 1944 [www.pearlharborwebsite.com]. Many prestigious Oklahomans attended the memorial dedication in Hawaii, including Jasmine and Melvin Moran, and several of the ship's survivors. Guest speakers included Hawaii Governor Linda Lingle; Oklahoma Governor Brad Henry; and Mary Fallin, at that time Congresswoman of Oklahoma [newsok.com]. Among those donating to the memorial, designed by Oklahoman Don Beck [www.beckdesign.com], were the Oklahoma Centennial Commission and many Oklahoma foundations, businesses and individuals.

Marci and Dale Donaho and Melvin and I were part of a group from Oklahoma who attended the USS *Oklahoma* memorial. It was the coldest summer Hawaii had in 100 years. Believe me when I say cold, I mean it. I come from England, cool to me was chilly, but this was COLD.

It was another of those times that I felt I shouldn't be going. I didn't feel well and I told Melvin I wasn't supposed to go. By now, I never deny something I have dreamed. I felt something was very wrong. And I probably should not have gone.

It was the first long trip after a lot of problems with my back.

It was giving me fits at the time. There were two ways of going, with the group or on our own. One of the groups was going on a plane that had these beds, almost like a hammock would be best description. It was fairly expensive to fly with these beds on this plane. Melvin and I are always conservative. We don't want to spend money we could donate to someone else. But because of the condition of my back and neck, we decided we would pay the extra fare.

We had just settled down. They gave us a drink starting out. We were going from Dallas completely to Honolulu. I climbed into the hammock and was just getting to "Lala Land" and it's lovely, I'm nearly there, when I hear the pilot say, "Ladies and gentlemen, I have some disturbing news. I don't want you to get worried but we're having a little problem in the cockpit and we are going to need to land in Los Angeles. We will land within 10 minutes so everybody be prepared to get off the plane. We are going to be met by ambulances and fire departments."

Everybody was looking at everybody else—most of us knew each other. I wondered if somebody carried a bomb onto the plane. The pilot said, "We will fly straight to the airport, but we will not be landing near a gate. There will be buses to take you to the terminal and they'll tell you the status of our flight to Honolulu."

Four hours later, we finally left on another plane. There were no nice hammocks on the second plane. Those who thought they were going to get a nice nap were wrong. I was so disappointed.

When we arrived in Honolulu, it was 2 in the morning. There was hardly anyone there except a lady with a lei around her neck. We were all exhausted. We all looked pretty haggard; I looked like one of the Beverly Hillbillies, I'm sure. My neck was in awful shape. This woman was actually there to meet our plane and take us to our bus. She apologized and tried to point out some of the sites as we drove through the almost empty streets, but we could barely see. It was dark.

When we arrived at the hotel, there was construction and no porters, so we had to walk a 10-minute hike uphill with our luggage. We were all so tired, it was an effort. At the desk, they upgraded our rooms, but we soon wished they had not.

Melvin said, "Let's wait until morning to unpack."

"No, I want to wear some of these things in the morning and they've already been in the bag for nearly 24 hours." Melvin wasn't happy, but I'm very picky about that. And when I hang things up, I want the shoulder seams the right way and all that stuff. So unpack I did.

We finally got into bed an hour later and I was once again in Lala Land for about two hours, when suddenly I heard, "Bang, bang, bang and bang." There was a five-minute pause, then "Bang, bang, bang, bang, bang." Melvin came to and said, "Is that you?"

I said, "Good heavens no."

He asked, "Is someone banging on the door?"

"No, I can't figure out what it is." It sounded like metal balls rolling across a floor. I said, "Do you suppose there are kids upstairs or do you think there could be a bowling alley?"

It was about 5:30 or 6:00 a.m. We called the front desk and found they had put us in the part of the hotel under construction. We had to pack up our luggage and get downstairs. The noise continued only louder. It sounded like the whole place was being banged on. A man came with a trolley and took us two more buildings away.

The trip didn't get much better. It was freezing cold. I had to wear almost everything in my suitcase at the same time.

It was because of the bad weather that we found Hawaii's children's museum, the Hawaii Children's Discovery Center, in Honolulu. They weren't going to let us in because we were not

Melvin and Jasmine were exhausted and freezing when they got to Hawaii to attend the dedication of the USS *Oklahoma* memorial. Their trip also included a memorable visit to the Hawaii Children's Discovery Center.

accompanied by children. We were an elderly couple coming in, and they couldn't reason why we would want to come see a children's museum. They asked if we had family with us and we said no. We wondered if they were going to take our fingerprints before we could get in. Finally they said we could come to the front desk to discuss entry.

We arrived at the front desk and explained that we were in Hawaii for the reception for the USS *Oklahoma*. We gave them our names and they spelled them very carefully. They wanted our full address. We were facing this woman at the desk who was asking us all these questions and we were wondering why, then an arm comes between Melvin and me, and there is a photograph on the end in the hand. It's a picture of Melvin with this lady. A voice behind us said, "I started the Hawaii Children's Discovery Center here and your husband was so gracious when we came to Oklahoma to see your museum. We asked if we could take a photo with him and he agreed. You are very welcome guests." Loretta Yajima is the chairman of the board of directors there and is still inspiring children 30 years after beginning the museum. She was very, very gracious and took us throughout the museum personally. We enjoyed the time we had there. The museum was very well done.

Really amazing things have happened to us.

The dedication of the USS *Oklahoma* was inspiring. People had undergone terrible things, bombs and fire; they didn't know if they were going to survive. They were diving into flames to get off the ship. We heard amazing stories from people who had actually survived this terrible ordeal. We were glad we went, but the bad weather and the cancelled flight were clearly the reasons for my feeling that we weren't supposed to go. Luckily the worst that happened was that I got sick when we flew back into Dallas in an ice storm, had to take a train to Oklahoma City, and got stranded without our luggage at the Colcord Hotel. Everyone was so kind to us at the hotel and made us comfortable for the night. Melvin was able to pick up our car in the morning while I stayed at the hotel. Our lost luggage was returned by the airport valet the next day. But I was as sick as a dog for the rest of the week.

IN RETROSPECT

Chapter 30

In my life, there have been so many people to inspire me: Mother Theresa gave up her life to take care of the sick. Winston Churchill got us through some very bad times: "We will fight them on the beaches, etc..." He gave us the right spirit, that we weren't going to war to kill, but to prevent killing and to prevent further anguish. Some call him a war monger, but he wasn't. If it hadn't been for his courage and encouragement of the British people, I'm not sure England would still be the England that I knew.

Churchill inspired us. Current leaders don't inspire and are without inspiration for themselves. I am somewhat discouraged by what I see today. Inspiration develops courage. Franklin Roosevelt was a wonderful man, Harry Truman, even Dwight Eisenhower had his moments. And Abraham Lincoln, what would this country be without him? I often wonder if I shouldn't have lived during his time. I've had so many adventures and met many inspiring people. I guess I'm as happy as I will ever be with my thoughts and memories.

My role models: Phyllis Calvert was a big movie star like Angelina Jolie and she played the title character in the stage version of *Peter Pan*, while I was Liza, the maid in the show, only 13 years old.

On opening night, she came out and spoke to the cast, telling us to just do our best, we were all new kids in the show and to just comfort each other if anything went wrong. She was so kind and took time to reassure each of us of her faith in us. She was the type of person everybody looked up to. She would always take the time out of her day to say things like, "The show was good last night" and "You did an especially wonderful speech" or whatever. You always think of the star as being above everyone and out of touch, but she was a real person who was revered by everyone.

Peter Murrey-Hill, her husband, played Captain Hook in the movie, and they were both just lovely people. I've been blessed to work with such nice people. We put these people on pedestals and many are not worthy, but these two were.

People who have made a big difference in my life: Gene Rainbolt and his wife were so kind to Melvin and so supportive of our dreams and ideas and always did anything we asked of them, including helping with the Children's Museum. Robert Henry has had many fundraising

Actress Phyllis Calvert signed this photo for Jasmine: "Best wishes for a successful future." She inspired Jasmine with her down-to-earth goodness.

dinners in his home to support the museum and introduced us to so many people who have helped us. David Boren and his lovely wife Molly have been most helpful, taking us to places and telling people about the museum in our presence to get support for us. They too have been most generous in their donations to the museum and have been great friends. We have been blessed with so many kind and understanding friends, who have a genuine interest in helping to create something good for the state.

I met George Nigh years ago when he was teaching at East Central University. We were both shopping in the same store and he was buying a beautiful slip. I asked if it was for his girlfriend or his wife and he said it was for a girlfriend. I said, "Well, she will have to marry you after you give her a beautiful petticoat like that." He said, "You don't miss much do you?" He has such a whacko sense of humor and still does today. He has been a very good friend and was a wonderful governor and leader for the state of Oklahoma. He has spoken at many of our Children's Museum banquets.

In a list of people who inspire me, I have to add my dear friends, Marci

Melvin and Jasmine have been close friends with Robert and Jan Henry for many years. Their relationship began when Jasmine played Robert's mother-in-law in *A Man for All Seasons*.

The Morans with David and Molly Boren. Their decades-long friendship began when David was a debate student at Seminole High School.

Donna and George Nigh, center, were winners of the museum's Jasmine Award, which recognizes an Oklahoman who has done positive things for children. They are pictured with the Morans, left, and Governor Brad Henry and his wife, Kim.

and Dale Donaho. Under Marci's direction, the Children's Museum has become more than anything we ever believed. And in those years, Marci and Dale have become more than just friends. I love them dearly.

I once met Henry Kissinger, but only for a moment. We were at a dinner and he was Secretary of State. David Boren had brought him as our guest speaker. After his speech, Melvin wanted to stay and meet Mr. Kissinger and Junior Phillips would wait there with him. Isla Mae Phillips and I needed the ladies' room. The one on that floor was full of people, so we were going down to the next floor. The staircase was full of people, so I said, "Let's just take the elevator."

I pushed the elevator button and the doors slid open and there stood Henry Kissinger with two security guards. Isla Mae and I both

Jasmine embraces her dear friend, Marci Donaho. The Morans believe Marci's dedication to The Children's Museum matches their own.

Jasmine and her friend Isla Mae Phillips once met Henry Kissinger in an elevator. The one-flight trip made an impact the two Seminole residents didn't soon forget.

went, "Blink blink." He leaned forward and smiled and said, "Are you lovely ladies going to let me ride the elevator down by myself?" And suddenly we were thrust forward, a surge of people pushing us into the elevator. The two of us almost fell down, pushed by all those behind us. Isla Mae and I flattened the two body guards and Mr. Kissinger against the back wall. I lost my shoe, a strappy sandal, and I had to find it before I could leave the elevator. I was fumbling all around the floor for it and finally someone handed it to me.

Henry Kissinger was so taken aback when the whole crowd came rushing at him. There were about 20 people in there by the time the door closed, all crushed up together. I wish I had a photograph; his face was one of horror. We really were coming at him about 90 miles per hour, about to fall. He put his arms up. Isla Mae said she didn't know how she kept her balance. She said she probably took the air out of the security guard, but he was so nice. They just stood against the back wall and nobody said a word. Thank goodness it was just one floor or I would have suffocated. I never looked back or apologized.

When Isla Mae and I came out of the elevator, both of us looked disheveled, with our clothes all twisted, our lipstick all smeared. I will never forget the panicked look Kissinger gave us as we descended upon him. That was my one and only experience with Henry Kissinger, having my face buried in his tux. It was definitely a Lucille Ball moment.

Joseph Jacobson was one of the founders of Israel and served as the war minister for Golda Meir. He was admired by many, including me. To be in his presence was an honor. He was so very tolerant of all people and very skilled in politics. Rich or poor,

Melvin became friends with Joseph Jacobson, a founder of Israel. He visited the Morans in Seminole and they visited him in his country.

religious or non-religious, he inspired everyone. He is another that some people call a man of war, but he was not. He hated war, which is such a destructive act.

We met him when he visited Tulsa in 1980 and became good friends for the rest of his life. He came here as a representative of Israel and visited us in Seminole. When we traveled to Israel, he would pick us up at the airport in a limousine. He arranged for us to have a beautiful suite in the historic King David Hotel, with a big cake that said "Welcome to Israel." There were flowers and a massive bowl of fruit, nuts, and cheese. I told Melvin we were in the wrong room. But we weren't. This was all done by Mr. Jacobson to make us feel comfortable and welcome.

Joseph Jacobson was a very fine man, well educated and also well liked by the Arabs. He took us to visit one of his friends, an Arab chief. We went to the chief's tent, which was enormous, as big as our whole house. He didn't live there but it was ceremonial for visitors. They always say, "Welcome to my humble home." Believe me, there was nothing humble about this tent. It was big and billowy with Persian rugs everywhere. Velvet cushions lay in big heaps in the seating area. The carpets were all beautifully hand-woven. There were small tables to sit and lounge at. His staff served us a splendid meal. The serving people were both men and women. The men brought liquids, the women brought meats. There were big plates of figs and dates and numerous exotic fruits. It was all beautifully done like in an Arabian movie. The women wore brassiere tops with puffy sleeves and billowy pants and the men dressed in beautifully colored vests with billowing shirts underneath and turban hats. Mr. Jacobson said that if we didn't like the taste of something, just put it back on the plate with no comment. The tea was very sweet. They put about two and a half teaspoons of sugar in a tiny demitasse cup. My eyes almost crossed and

I tried not to gasp. I drank the tea and all the sugar almost did me in. I will never forget feeling so at ease in the company of both an Arab and Jew. Mr. Jacobson and this man were obviously very good friends. It was a fascinating afternoon.

I have so many memories of my trips to Israel and all of them have been wonderful experiences. I have never been fearful, though it is considered by many to be dangerous. Sometimes I have felt safer there than in parts of the United States. I have always regarded Israel as a country of many religions and wished all could come together in peace and tranquility. Over the years, and I have been there eight times now, I have seen many changes, but I never feel fearful in Israel.

There is a beautiful song, "Jerusalem of Gold." It became well known by servicemen, who sang as they fought for their country. They used it as an anthem. Mr. Jacobson had heard it sung and said, "You must learn this song and I think you will learn to love it as much as I do. You will remember this song for the rest of your life," and I have.

The olive trees that stand in silence upon the hills of Time,
To hear the voices of the city as bells of evening chime.
The shofar (ram's horn blown in Israel during Jewish religious services)
sounding from the temple to call the world to prayer,
The shepherd pauses in the valley and peace is everywhere.
Jerusa-lem, Jerusa-lem, oh city with the heart of gold
My heart will sing your songs of glory.
Jerusa-lem Jerusa-lem, Jerusa-lem
Forever young, yet forever old
My heart will sing your songs of glory Jerusa-lem.
The water well for those who thirsted, the ancient market square,
Your golden sun that lights the future for all men everywhere.
How many songs, how many stories, the ancient hills recall.

Around her heart my city carries, a lonely ancient wall.

Jerusa-lem, Jerusa-lem, the city with the heart of gold

My heart will sing your songs of glory.

Jerusa-lem, Jerusa-lem,

Forever young but forever old

The city with a heart of gold,

My heart will sing your songs of glory

Jerusa-lem.

And away beyond the dessert, a thousand suns will glow,

We shall be going to the Jordan by way of Jericho.

My simple voice cannot acclaim thee,

 Too weak the words I choose.

Jerusa-lem, Jerusa-lem

If I forget thee,

May my right hand its cunning lose.

Jerusa-lem, Jerusa-lem,

The city with the heart of gold,

Forever young yet forever old,

My heart will sing your songs of glory

Jerusa-lem.

You can just see in your mind the soldiers going off for the Six Day War, singing this song and wondering if they will ever be back. Once we were traveling with friends from California, and as we approached Jerusalem in the mini tour bus, I asked our Israeli driver if he knew the song. He laughed and said, "I think everyone here does." He sang it in Hebrew as I sang in English. We sat in this beautiful sunset looking down from the hills on Jerusalem singing this moving song. Jerusalem was sparkling. Our friend who was with us, Donna Terry, said it brought tears to her eyes. It is such a beautiful memory.

Poets and painters inspired me all my life with new ideas. Appropriately, perhaps, my favorite poem is Robert Browning's "Home Thoughts from Abroad."

Oh, to be in England
Now that April's there,
And whoever wakes in England
Sees, some morning, unaware,

All these people and places have left a little residue on me. They have given me inspiration to try to improve what I can. When I can't improve anything, I just do the best I can.

My private life is very, very private. Sharing it bothers me some, though I've never done anything I'm ashamed of. When I've done something and realized it wasn't right, I always went back and apologized. I never made any excuse for leaving something in the lurch. You go back and humble yourself, no matter what, and I always do. If necessary you must make restitution.

I have been truly blessed. I came into this world with so many strikes against me. You'd think I would never amount to a hill of beans. I was dyslexic. My parents were separated, on the verge of divorce. My mother had difficulty saying the word love. She never said it, not even when she died. But we were well aware that she loved us.

Jasmine and Melvin remained close with her family despite the long distance between them for the rest of their lives. Here they sit for a portrait with sister Davina and mom Lilian in her later years.

I was in a role I never thought I'd have: first show business, then raising my three children. Because they have dedicated their lives to helping others, I proudly believe they are my most significant contribution to society.

I was named Seminole's Citizen of the Year in 2000 and, with Melvin, received a Founder's Award from Seminole State College in 2004, for funding several endowed nursing scholarships. These accolades have been such highlights in my life.

I have been blessed by the fine children that Melvin and I have raised, all of whom have made significant contributions to the areas in which they live: Indiana, Colorado and Michigan. And I see my grandchildren following in the footsteps of their parents. They are my reward and my legacy to the future.

Jasmine was named Citizen of the Year by her hometown of Seminole, Oklahoma. Celebrating her achievement are husband Melvin, daughters Elisa and Marilyn, and son-in-law Bill Townsend.

Life is like a flower. For a long time, the bulb is in the ground, then it shoots up green leaves, and then a daffodil or tulip blooms, and it brings perfume and color to the world for however long God wants. Then it fades and dies. I hope I give joy like that; not everyone does. When we fade, it's time to leave and someone will replace us.

Another way to think of it is like the butterfly. The cocoon opens, the butterfly begins moving and takes to the air. It gives a lot of joy until it dies.

I've often wondered what I might do differently, but I think I would do everything exactly the same. Would I go back? No. Good heavens no. I've earned my wrinkles and gray hair. Now I just want to sit back and try to enjoy them. I think I found the right path.

Melvin and Jasmine are considered the "first family" of Seminole by many residents, despite the fact that Melvin's service as mayor was years ago. They both continue to stay active in community events.

Jasmine and Melvin are now the matriarch and patriarch of their growing family. As they get older, it becomes more difficult for them to travel to family gatherings. Here they are surrounded by their three children and their spouses, children, and grandchildren.

BIBLIOGRAPHY

Page 2 – Way, George and Squire, Romilly. *Clans & Tartan*, New York: HarperCollins, 1996.

Page 5 – Sharpe, Gillian. "The Role of Scottish Women in the Suffragette Movement." *www.bbc.com/news/uk-scotland-34489496*. 10 October, 2015. Web. Accessed 22 July 2017.

Page 9 – "Queen Elizabeth the Queen Mother." (no author or date listed) *www.royal.uk/queen-elizabeth-queen-mother*. Web. Accessed 22 July 2017.

Page 12 – *www.flyingscotsman.org.uk/about*. (no author or date listed) Web. Accessed 22 July 2017.

Page 30 – "RAF Hornchurch." (no date or author listed) *www.pastcape. org.uk*. Web. Historic England. Accessed 22 July 2017.

Page 31 – Taylor, Robert. "Hornchurch Scramble: The Hardest Days Part II." *www.brooksart.com/hornchurch.html*. Brooks Aviation Art. Web. Accessed 23 July 2017.

Page 31 – Royde-Smith, John Graham. "World War II 1939-1945." *www.britannica.com/event/world-war-II*. Encyclopaedia Britannica. Updated 18 July 2017. Web. Accessed 22 July, 2017.

Page 36 – Churchill, Winston. "We Shall Fight on the Beaches" speech. *www.winstonchurchill.org/resources/speeches/1940-the-finest-hour/we-shall-fight-on-the-beaches*. International Churchill Society. 4 June 1940. Web. Accessed 22 July 2017

Page 38 – "The London Blitz, 1940." *www.eyewitnesstohistory.com*. Eyewitness to History. 2001. Web. Accessed 22 July 2017.

Page 45 – Reid, John D. "WW2 British Child Evacuees to Canada." *www.johndreid.com/home/ww2-british-child-evacuees-to-canada*. (No publication date listed) Web. Accessed 22 July 2017.

Page 46 – Photo courtesy the Royal Navy. "77 Children Lost With City of Benares." *ww2today/17th/september-1940-77-children-lost-with-city-of-benares*. World War II Today – Follow the War As It Happened. Copyrighted 2008-2017. Web. Accessed 22 July 2017.

Page 47 – Wilson, Lt. Col. G.R.S. "Report on the Collision Which Occurred on 17th April 1948 at Winsford in the London Midland Region British Railways." *www.railways archive.co.uk*. 30 July 1948. Railways Archive ... Opening Up British Rail History. Crown copyright and database rights 2017. Web. Accessed 22 July, 2017.

Page 65 – Armand, C.M. "Brief History of Consolidated B24 Bomber." *modelismo.wehrmacht-info.com/consolidated-b-24-j-liberator-1144-academy-modelismo*. (no date available). Web. Accessed 22 July 2017.

Page 66 – Bundesarchiv, Bild 146-1973-029A-24A. *en.wikipedia.org/ wiki/v-1-flying-bomb#/media/BundesarchiveBild146-1973-029A-24A.* 31 December 1943. Web. Accessed 22 July 2017

Page 67 – U.S. Air Force. *www.nationalmuseum.af.mil/shared/media/ photodb/photos/ 060515-F-1234S-018.jpg.* From www.wikipedia.com. Web. Accessed 22 July 2017.

Page 81 – Overy, Richard. "Civilians on the Front Line: Second World War." *The Guardian.* 6 September 2009. *www.theguardian.com/ world/2009/sep/06/blitz-second-world-war.* Web. Accessed 23 July 2017.

Page 81 – Wood, Hunter. "How the Blitz Affected Civilian Morale in London." *prezi.com/zk0ghzyxyfgn/how-the-blitz-affected-civilian-morale-in-london.* Prezi. 3 May 2016. Web. Accessed 23 July 2017.

Page 81 – Roberts, Andrew. "Britain at War: The Blitz and the Home Front." *The Telegraph.* 22 October 2008. *www.telegraph.co.uk/history/ britain-at-war/3240659/Britain-at-war-The-Blitz-and-the-Home-Front.html.* Web. Accessed 23 July 2017.

Pages 84 – History.com staff. "This Day in History: Dunkirk Evacuation Ends." *www.history.com/this-day-in-history/dunkirk-evacuation-ends.* A+E Networks. 4 June 2010. Web. 24 July 2017.

Page 84-85 – Axe, David. "Exposed: How Close Nazi Germany Came to Invading Britain (And the One Thing That Stopped Them." *nationalinterest.org/blog/the-buzz/exposed-how-close-Nazi-Germany-Came-Invading-Britain-the-one-18160.* The National Interest. 24 October 2016. Web. Accessed 25 July 2017.

Page 103 – "Michael Medwin Biography." *www.imdb.com/name/ nm0575974/bio*. Amazon. IMDb.com Inc. Copyright 1990-2017. Web. Accessed 25 July 2017.

Page 112 – Trueman, C.N. "Archibald McIndoe and the Guinea Pig Club." *historylearningsite.co.uk*. The History Learning Site. 21 May 2015. Web. Accessed 25 July 2017.

Page 138 – Spivack, Emily. "Stocking Series, Part 1: Wartime Rationing and Nylon Riots." *Smithsonianmag.com*. Smithsonian Institute. 4 September 2012. Web. Accessed 25 July 2017

Page 148-149 – Fox, Mark. *Through the Stage Door Theatre Royal Drury Lane Resource Book*. London: Centurion Press Limited. 1999. Print.

Page 150 – "Millicent Martin Biography." *www.imdb.com/name/ nm0552815/bio*. Amazon. IMDb.com Inc. Copyright 1990-2017. Web. Accessed 28 July 2017.

Page 153 – "Muriel Smith Biography." *www.imdb.com/name/ nm0809421/bio*. Amazon. IMDb.com Inc. Copyright 1990-2017. Web. Accessed 28 July 2017.

Page 154 – "Wilbur "Wib" Evans Biography." *www.imdb.com/name/ nm0263305/bio*. Amazon. IMDb.com Inc. Copyright 1990-2017. Web. Accessed 28 July 2017.

Page 155 – "Mary Martin Biography." *www.imdb.com/name/ nm0552756/bio*. Amazon. IMDb.com Inc. Copyright 1990-2017. Web. Accessed 28 July 2017.

Page 155 – Holden, Stephen. "Julie Wilson, Sultry Cabaret Legend and Actress, Dies at 90." *www.nytimes.com/2015/04/07/arts/music/julie-wilson-sultry-cabaret-legend-and-actress-dies-at-90*. New York Times. 6 April 2015. Web. Accessed 28 July, 2017.

Page 156 – *www.larryhagman.com/biography*. 22 July 2015. Web. Accessed 28 July 2017.

Page 157 – *www.rnh.com/rodgers and hammerstein/full_bio*. Imagem Publishing Group. Web. Accessed 28 July 2017.

Page 201 – *www.gov/ky/portal/page/portal/cighome/government/formofgovernment*. 11 June 2009. Web. Accessed 28 July 2017

Page 221 – Biography.com editors. "Russell Means Biography." *biography.com/people/russell-means-21016231*. A&E Television Network. 13 February 2015. Web. Accessed 28 July 2017.

Page 244 – *www.pearlharborwebsite.com/pearl-harbor/tours/itinerary/uss-Oklahoma-memorial*. 2015-2017. Web. Accessed 28 July 2017.

Page 244 – McCoy, Audrey. "USS Oklahoma: Remembering." *newsok.com/article/2982863*. Newsok.com. 8 Dec. 2006. Updated 5 October 2007. Web Accessed 28 July 2017.

Page 244 – "USS Oklahoma Memorial." *www.beckdesign.com/uss-oklahoman-memorial*. Web. Accessed 28 July 2017.

INDEX

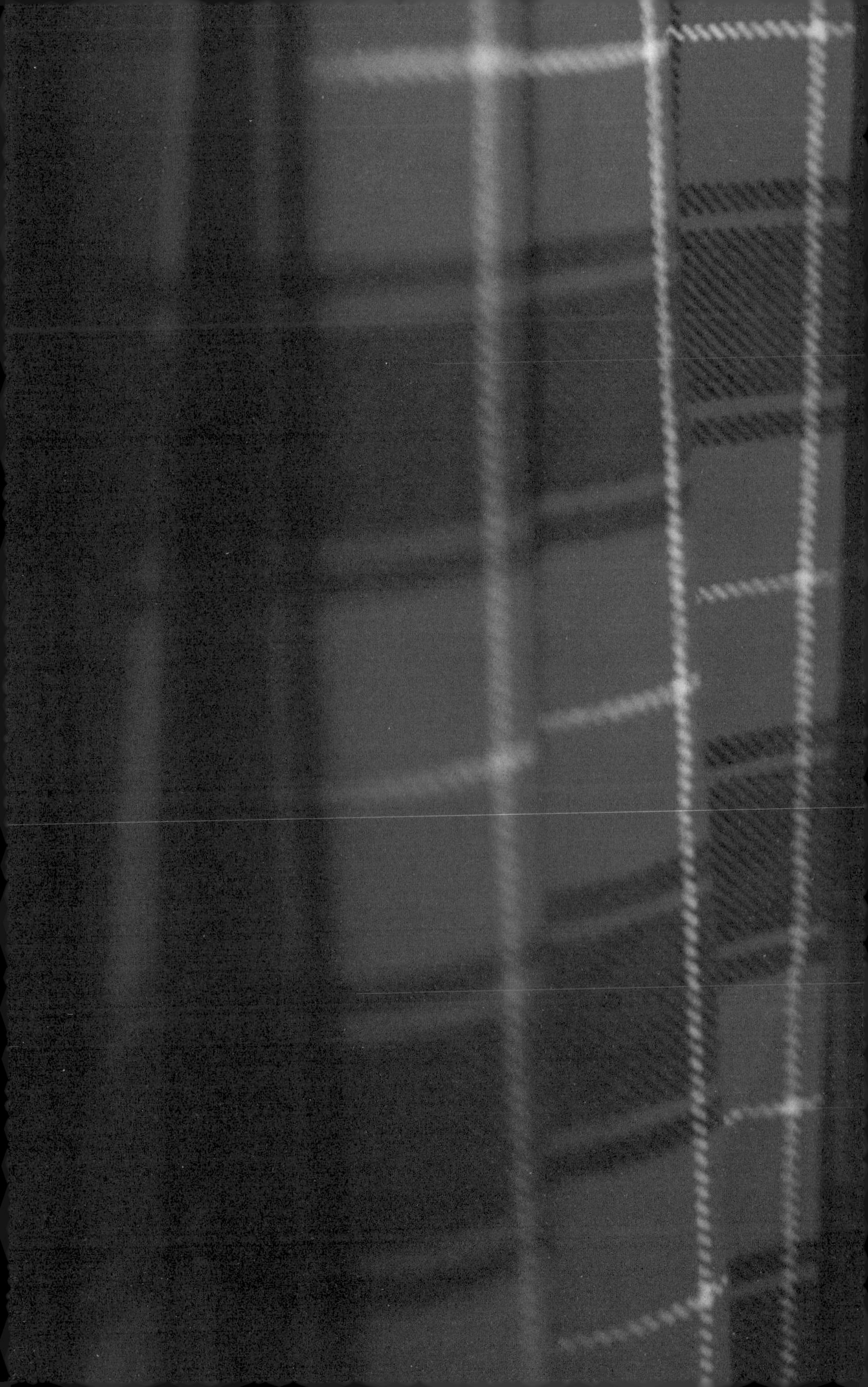